COSORI AIR FRYER COOKBOOK UK

1500 Days Easy and Effortless Recipes to Enjoy Delicious Foods In a Healthier Way Using Your Favorite Air Fryer

Nicholas Landry

Table of Contents

INTRODUCTION 4
- What is a Cosori Air Fryer? 4
- How Does It Work? 5
- Cosori Air Fryer Features 5
- Benefits of Cosori Air Fryer 6
- How To Use a Cosori Air Fryer 7
- Using the Preset Air Frying Programs 7
- How to Clean a Cosori Air Fryer? 9
- Tips on Using the Cosori Air Fryer 10

CHAPTER 1: BREAKFAST RECIPES 12
1. Roasted Pepper Egg Bite 12
2. Cheese Sausage Egg Muffins 12
3. Green Chilis Egg Bite 12
4. Cheddar Cheese Broccoli Egg Bite 13
5. Broccoli Bell Pepper Frittata 13
6. Gruyere Cheese Egg Bite 13
7. Bacon Cheese Egg Bites 14
8. Cheese Omelet 14
9. Cheese Sausage Pepper Frittata 14
10. Cheese Ham Egg Cups 15
11. Healthy Spinach Omelet 15
12. Breakfast Radish Hash Browns 15
13. Classic Sweet Potato Hash 16
14. Mushroom Frittata 16
15. Breakfast Cream Souffle 16
16. Cheese Mushroom Egg Bake 17
17. Spinach Tomato Frittata 17
18. Easy Cheesy Breakfast Eggs 17
19. Cheesy Chicken Fritters 18
20. Ham Egg Bites 18
21. Delicious Chicken Burger Patties 18
22. Cheese Egg Frittata 19
23. Breakfast Avocado Eggs 19
24. Basil Feta Egg Bite 19
25. Sausage Swiss Cheese Egg Bite 19

CHAPTER 2: VEGETABLE RECIPES 21
26. Curried Eggplant Slices 21
27. Balsamic Brussels Sprouts 21
28. Simple Vegan Broccoli 21
29. Easy & Crisp Brussels Sprouts 21
30. Asparagus with Almonds 22
31. Garlicky Cauliflower Florets 22
32. Air Fryer Basil Tomatoes 22
33. Easy Roasted Vegetables 23

34. Easy Roasted Carrots 23
35. Curried Cauliflower with Pine Nuts 23
36. Spiced Green Beans 24
37. Parmesan Brussels sprouts 24
38. Air Fryer Ratatouille 24
39. Flavorful Tomatoes 25
40. Healthy Mixed Vegetables 25
41. Healthy Roasted Carrots 25
42. Healthy Squash & Zucchini 25
43. Garlic Green Beans 26
44. Asian Broccoli 26
45. Crunchy Fried Cabbage 26

CHAPTER 3: CHICKEN AND POULTRY 27
46. Perfect Chicken Thighs Dinner 27
47. Flavors Dijon Chicken 27
48. Nutritious Chicken & Veggies 27
49. Turkey Spinach Patties 28
50. Perfectly Spiced Chicken Tenders 28
51. Perfect Chicken Breasts 28
52. Tasty Turkey Fajitas 29
53. Lemon Pepper Turkey Breast 29
54. Juicy Chicken Breasts 29
55. Healthy Chicken & Broccoli 30
56. Tender Turkey Legs 30
57. Chicken Spinach Meatballs 31
58. Flavorful Chicken Tenders 31
59. Juicy Lemon Pepper Chicken Thighs ... 32
60. Flavors & Crisp Chicken Thighs 32
61. Creamy Pesto Chicken 32
62. Greek Meatballs 33
63. Crispy Crusted Chicken Tenders 33
64. Quick & Easy Lemon Pepper Chicken . 33
65. Tender & Juicy Cornish Hens 33

CHAPTER 4: FISH AND SEAFOODS 35
66. Garlic Yogurt Salmon Fillets 35
67. Old Bay Shrimp 35
68. Lemon Garlic White Fish 35
69. Juicy & Tender Cod Fillets 36
70. Healthy Crab Cakes 36
71. Lime Garlic Shrimp Kababs 36
72. Tasty Chipotle Shrimp 37
73. Perfectly Tender Frozen Fish Fillets 37
74. Ginger Garlic Salmon 37
75. Flavorful Parmesan Shrimp 37

- 76. Crisp Bacon Wrapped Scallops 38
- 77. Chili Lime Cod 38
- 78. Simple & Perfect Shrimp 39
- 79. Tasty Shrimp Fajitas 39
- 80. Parmesan White Fish Fillets 39
- 81. Delicious Fish Bites 40
- 82. Healthy Salmon Patties 40
- 83. Old Bay Seasoned Crab Cakes 40
- 84. Quick & Easy Salmon 41
- 85. Asian Salmon Steak 41

CHAPTER 5: MEAT 42

- 86. Tasty Ginger Garlic Beef 42
- 87. Easy Greek Lamb Chops 42
- 88. Garlicky Beef & Broccoli 42
- 89. Creole Seasoned Pork Chops 43
- 90. Dash Seasoned Pork Chops 43
- 91. Moist Lamb Roast 43
- 92. Quick & Easy Lamb Chops 43
- 93. Delicious Zaatar Lamb Chops 44
- 94. Cheese Garlicky Pork Chops 44
- 95. Baked Lamb Chops 44
- 96. Cheese Butter Steak 45
- 97. Tasty Steak Fajitas 45
- 98. Crispy Pork Chops 45
- 99. Herb Cheese Pork Chops 46
- 100. Thyme Lamb Chops 46
- 101. Flavorful Beef Roast 46
- 102. Garlic Lemon Pork Chops 47
- 103. Coconut Butter Pork Chops 47
- 104. Flavors Burger Patties 47
- 105. Tender Pork Chops 48
- 106. Lime Cumin Beef 48
- 107. Dried Herb Lamb Chops 48
- 108. Asian Pork Chops 49
- 109. Easy & Delicious Pork Chops 49
- 110. Steak with Mushrooms 49

CHAPTER 6: SNACKS AND APPETIZERS 51

- 111. Crispy Zucchini Fries 51
- 112. Cheese Stuffed Mushrooms 51
- 113. Ranch Zucchini Chips 51
- 114. Healthy Jicama Fries 52
- 115. Easy Broccoli Nuggets 52
- 116. Easy Jalapeno Poppers 52
- 117. Herb Roasted Carrots 53
- 118. Healthy Zucchini Chips 53
- 119. Delicious Chicken Dip 53
- 120. Stuffed Jalapeno Poppers 53
- 121. Simple Air Fried Vegetables 54
- 122. Flavorful Eggplant Slices 54
- 123. Spicy Salmon Bites 54
- 124. Crab Stuffed Mushrooms 55
- 125. Crispy Brussels sprouts 55
- 126. Crispy Cauliflower Bites 55
- 127. Healthy Roasted Almonds 56
- 128. Healthy Roasted Pecans 56
- 129. Chicken Stuffed Poblanos 56
- 130. Parmesan Carrot Fries 56

CHAPTER 7: DESSERTS 58

- 131. Almond Butter Fudge Brownies 58
- 132. Delicious Chocó Cookies 58
- 133. Yummy Brownie Muffins 58
- 134. Blueberry Muffins 59
- 135. Cinnamon Cappuccino Muffins 59
- 136. Almond Cookies 59
- 137. Vanilla Almond Cinnamon Mug Cake 60
- 138. Lemon Cheese Muffins 60
- 139. Choco Almond Butter Brownie 60
- 140. Butter Cookies 61
- 141. Choco Mug Brownie 61
- 142. Lemon Ricotta Cake 61
- 143. Delicious Chocolate Muffins 62
- 144. Chocolate Protein Brownie 62
- 145. Cream Cheese Brownies 62
- 146. Mozzarella Cheese Butter Cookies 63
- 147. Moist Almond Muffins 63
- 148. Vanilla Custard 63
- 149. Vanilla Mug Cake 64
- 150. Cheesecake Muffins 64

CONVERSION CHART 65

30-DAY MEAL PLAN 67

INDEX 69

CONCLUSION 71

Introduction

Air fryers have made oil-free cooking a reality, and today there are millions of people around the world who rely on this technology to cook all sorts of oil-free healthy meals at home.

Cosori has emerged as a trusted air fryer manufacturer over the years; the cooking technology and the user interface used in the appliances created by Cosori have garnered much appreciation and positive reviews from its customers. And when it comes to recommending an air fryer for every household, the multipurpose Cosori Air Fryer always comes to mind.

The reason is the ease and comfort of cooking and the effective results it offers. You will not be disappointed with its cooking functions. So here comes a Cosori Air Fryer Cookbook which has a complete range of Cosori cooked meals.

What is a Cosori Air Fryer?

A Cosori Air Fryer is similar to an oven in the sense that it bakes and roasts, but the difference is its heating elements are only located on top and are accompanied by a large, powerful fan, resulting in food that's super crispy in no time — and, most notably, with less oil than deep-fried counterparts. Cosori Air Fryer typically heat up very quickly and they cook food quickly and evenly, thanks to the combination of a concentrated heat source and the size and placement of the fan.

How Does It Work?

The technology of the Cosori air fryer is very simple. Fried foods get their crunchy texture because hot oil heats foods quickly and evenly on their surface. Oil is an excellent heat conductor, which helps with fast and simultaneous cooking across all of the ingredients. For decades cooks have used convection ovens to try to mimic the effects of frying or cooking the whole surface of the food. But the air never circulates quickly enough to achieve that delicious surface crisp we all love in fried foods.

With this mechanism, the air is circulated on high degrees, up to 200° C, to "air fry" any food such as fish, chicken or chips, etc. This technology has changed the whole idea of cooking by reducing the fat up to 80% compared to old-fashioned deep fat frying.

The Cosori air fryer cooking releases the heat through a heating element which cooks the food in a healthier and more appropriate way.

There's also an exhaust fan right above the cooking chamber which provides the food required airflow. This way food is cooked with constant heated air. This leads to the same heating temperature reaching every single part of the food that is being cooked. So, this is only grill and the exhaust fan that is helping the Cosori air fryer to boost air at a constantly high speed in order to cook healthy food with less fat.

The internal pressure increases the temperature that will then be controlled by the exhaust system. Exhaust fan also releases filtered extra air to cook the food in a much healthier way. Cosori air fryer has no odor at all and it is absolutely harmless making it user and environment-friendly.

Cosori Air Fryer Features

Why I would like to introduce the air fryer of this brand? It is because I have used this air fryer for 3 months. Its many features and advantages have brought me great convenience and fun. Those features will make you love it better.

Highly Portable:

Designed to easily be transferred from your kitchen storage cabinet to the countertop or to and from any place in your home – making it great to take to a friend for a cook-off.

Cooking Presets:

This is the silver bullet of air fryers repertoire as it completely eliminates the need to set cooking times and temperatures for your commonly cooked foods. Ingredient specifications are preprogrammed into the appliance an all you have to do is choose the correct one, and with the push of a button the preset has got you covered.

Digital Touch Screen:

No need to have to learn about complicated cooking maneuvers or have master culinary skills to use your air fryer. Simplicity is inbuilt with this feature. Most models allow you to set your cooking preferences with just a few taps on the touch panel's screen and voila, you are good to go.

Automatic Temperature control:

Get a perfectly cooked food every time. Just set your air fryer to your desired temperature and you can be assured that it will effortlessly cook your food to the desired doneness.

Timer and buzzer:

No need to worry about having to constantly keep an eye on your food or about accidentally overcooking it. With this feature, you are frequently given audio cues on the progress of your meal.

Benefits of Cosori Air Fryer

Besides providing us comfort and satisfaction, eating fried foods provide little benefits. But with COSORI air fryer, anyone can whip up healthy and satisfying foods minus any guilt. There are many benefits of air frying your food instead of cooking them in a conventional deep fryer. Below are the benefits of why you should air fry your foods more often.

- **Versatile:** An air fryer is not only a fryer thus you can use it to cook different types of foods. You can use it to bake bread, make popcorn or even make roasted vegetables.
- **Cost effective:** Since you don't use any oil in cooking your food, you can save a lot of money from buying cooking oil.
- **Easy to cook:** Never mind if you are a kitchen novice. Since air fryers are digital, it requires less skill so you can cook delicious dishes even if you are not good at cooking.
- **Fewer calories:** Since you do not add any oil to cook your food compared to traditional frying methods, you don't add a few calories to cook your food. Remember that a cup of oil is already equivalent to 800 calories alone so deep frying increases the caloric value of your food to a dangerously high level.

The thing is that there are many benefits of air frying and if you decide to make a simple change in your diet by only eating fried foods that are cooked in an air fryer, you will be able to enjoy a healthier and more convenient life.

How To Use a Cosori Air Fryer

COSORI Air Fryer are equipped with buttons to help you prepare anything from grilling the perfect salmon to roasting an entire chicken or even baking a chocolate cake.

These buttons are programmed to preset times and temperatures based on your specific COSORI Air Fryer. Because of the wide variety of models on the market, all the recipes in this book were created using manual times and temperatures and with an automatic preheat function. If yours doesn't have this function, allow 5 minutes for preheating once you set the desired temperature.

Although the COSORI Air Fryer cooks with little to no oil, there are some cases in which a little spray is essential. Especially in recipes that involve breading and flour, like fried chicken, spritzing oil on the outside helps you get a brown and crispy exterior for a much tastier end product.

Using the Preset Air Frying Programs

Understanding how the pre-set cooking button works is very important so that you can cook food perfectly using your COSORI Air Fryer. The preset programs are programmed to cook food at ideal temperature and time. Below are the general steps when using pre-set cooking settings.

1. Preheat the air fryer. It is important to take note that the higher the cooking temperature, the longer the preheat setting. You can refer to your manual for the different preheat settings available for your COSORI Air Fryer.
2. Once the preheat temperature and time is achieved, the display will display the word "READY". This will be your cue to put your food in the basket.

3. Choose the desired pre-set cooking program. You can also customize the temperature and cooking time by pressing the Press Temp/Time button once. Click on either the + or – button to adjust the temperature. To change the time, Press the Temp/Time button a second time and press the + or – button to change the time. You can only cook your food for a maximum of 60 minutes.

4. Press the "Start" button to commence cooking. For some pre-set cooking settings, the Shake reminder will appear so be sure to flip the food halfway through the cooking time. Be careful of the hot steam when you take the cooking tray out. Do not press the Basket Release Button otherwise, the inner basket will fall. Once you are done flipping the food, put the basket back in the fryer.

5. Once the food is cooked, press the Keep Warm button so that the food is kept warm until you are ready to eat your food.

It is important to take note that the different pre-set cooking settings work differently and although the instructions are the same for using the pre-set acids, their specific settings are different. Below is a table showing the differences between the different pre-set cooking settings found in your COSORI Air Fryer.

Pre-Set Setting	Symbol	Default Temperature F/C	Default Time minutes	Shake Reminder
Steak		400/205	6	-
Chicken		380/193	25	-
Seafood		350/177	8	-
Shrimp		370/188	6	Shake
Bacon		320/160	8	-

Frozen Food		350/177	10	Shake
French Fries		380/193	25	Shake
Vegetables		300/149	10	Shake
Root Veggies		400/205	12	Shake
Bread		320/160	12	-
Dessert		300/149	8	-
Preheat		400/205	5	-
Keep Warm		170/77	5	-

How to Clean a Cosori Air Fryer?

Before cleaning it, first ensure that your COSORI Air Fryer is completely cool and unplugged. To clean the air fryer pan you'll need to:

6. Remove the air fryer pan from the base. Fill the pan with hot water and dish soap. Let the pan soak with the frying basket inside for 10 minutes.
7. Clean the basket thoroughly with a sponge or brush.
8. Remove the fryer basket and scrub the underside and outside walls.
9. Clean the air fryer pan with a sponge or brush.
10. Let everything air-dry and return to the air fryer base.

To clean the outside of your COSORI Air Fryer, simply wipe with a damp cloth. Then, be sure all components are in the correct position before beginning your next cooking adventure.

Tips on Using the Cosori Air Fryer

One of the best aspects of air frying is how simple it is to cook all your favorite foods. However, knowing a few tips and tricks will ensure that your air-fried food is perfect every time.

To make cleanup easier, use parchment paper.

For simpler cleanup, line the bottom of the air fryer baking pan or fryer basket with parchment paper. The parchment paper won't catch fire, but it will absorb much of the extra grease that may drip from fatty dishes.

To extend the life of your air fryer, keep it clean.

After each usage, clean the fryer basket and baking pan with a slightly moist paper towel or cloth for optimal results. For greasier things like meats or fish, as well as recipes with batter or breading, cleaning your air fryer may call for a little extra work. Your accessories can be soaked in warm, soapy water in these situations.

To minimize smoke, drain excess fat.

There is a risk of smoke escaping from the air fryer when fat drips and burns from meals like steak and chicken wings. If this happens, turn off the air fryer, gently drain the fat from the fryer basket, or pat any oily fat off the food with a paper towel, then quickly put the basket back in the air fryer and go on cooking.

Before cooking, preheat the air fryer.

When you insert the food into the air fryer, the temperature and airflow will already be at their ideal settings from the air fryer's preheating, which will help the food cook more evenly. This procedure may take 3 minutes (or less).

For breaded foods, use a baking pan.

Food fragments and small particles of breading may come loose and fly throughout the chamber because of the air fryer's air circulation. Cook food within the baking pan to avoid breading from coming undone. Using a baking pan can also stop food from falling apart and keep the air fryer clean.

To prevent uneven frying, shake the basket.

If you're having problems with uneven frying, the fryer basket is probably too crowded. During the cooking process, pause the air fryer once or twice (or as directed) and give the fryer basket a gentle shake for more equal frying. By redistributing the food, it will cook more uniformly and brown on all sides.

If used properly, the Cosori air fryer may produce surprisingly excellent food that is cooked in a way that is healthier than using a deep fryer or a conventional oven.

CHAPTER 1: Breakfast Recipes

1. Roasted Pepper Egg Bite

Preparation time: 10 minutes
Cooking time: 5 minutes
Servings: 7
Ingredients:

- 4 eggs
- 1/4 cup spinach, chopped
- 1/2 roasted red pepper, chopped
- 1 tbsp green onion, chopped
- 1/2 cup cottage cheese, crumbled
- 1/2 cup Monterey jack cheese, shredded
- Pepper
- Salt

Directions:

1. Spray egg mold with cooking spray and set aside.
2. In a bowl, beat eggs until frothy. Add remaining ingredients into the eggs and stir to mix.
3. Pour egg mixture into the prepared egg mold.
4. Place egg mold into the air fryer basket then cook at 330 F for 5 minutes.
5. Serve and enjoy.

Per serving: Calories: 82kcal; Fat: 5.3g; Carbs: 1.3g; Protein: 7.5g

2. Cheese Sausage Egg Muffins

Preparation time: 10 minutes
Cooking time: 5 minutes
Servings: 6
Ingredients:

- 4 eggs
- 4 tbsp cheddar cheese, shredded
- 2 tbsp heavy cream
- 1/2 cup cooked sausage
- Pepper
- Salt

Directions:

1. Spray egg mold with cooking spray and set aside.
2. In a bowl, beat eggs until frothy. Add remaining ingredients into the eggs and stir to mix.
3. Pour egg mixture into the prepared egg mold.
4. Place egg mold into the air fryer basket then cook at 330 F for 5 minutes.
5. Serve and enjoy.

Per serving: Calories: 82kcal; Fat: 6.6g; Carbs: 0.4g; Protein: 5.2g

3. Green Chilis Egg Bite

Preparation time: 10 minutes
Cooking time: 5 minutes
Servings: 7
Ingredients:

- 4 eggs
- 1/4 cup green chilis, diced
- 1/2 cup cottage cheese, crumbled
- 1/2 cup pepper jack cheese, shredded
- Pepper
- Salt

Directions:

1. Spray egg mold with cooking spray and set aside.
2. In a bowl, beat eggs until frothy. Add remaining ingredients into the eggs and stir to mix.
3. Pour egg mixture into the prepared egg mold.
4. Place egg mold into the air fryer basket then cook at 330 F for 5 minutes.
5. Serve and enjoy.

Per serving: Calories: 57kcal; Fat: 3.1g; Carbs: 1.4g; Protein: 5.5g

4. Cheddar Cheese Broccoli Egg Bite

Preparation time: 10 minutes
Cooking time: 5 minutes
Servings: 7
Ingredients:

- 4 eggs
- 1/4 cup broccoli, cooked and chopped
- 1/2 cup cottage cheese, crumbled
- 1/2 cup cheddar cheese, shredded
- Pepper
- Salt

Directions:

1. Spray egg mold with cooking spray and set aside.
2. In a bowl, beat eggs until frothy. Add remaining ingredients into the eggs and stir to mix.
3. Pour egg mixture into the prepared egg mold.
4. Place egg mold into the air fryer basket then cook at 330 F for 5 minutes.
5. Serve and enjoy.

Per serving: Calories: 84kcal; Fat: 5.5g; Carbs: 1.1g; Protein: 7.5g

5. Broccoli Bell Pepper Frittata

Preparation time: 10 minutes
Cooking time: 17 minutes
Servings: 2
Ingredients:

- 3 eggs
- 2 tbsp cheddar cheese, shredded
- 2 tbsp cream
- 1/2 cup bell pepper, chopped
- 1/2 cup broccoli florets, chopped
- 1/4 tsp garlic powder
- 1/4 tsp onion powder
- Pepper
- Salt

Directions:

1. Spray air fryer pan with cooking spray. Add bell peppers and broccoli into the pan.
2. Place pan in the air fryer basket then cook at 350 F for 7 minutes.
3. In a bowl, whisk eggs with cheese, cream, garlic powder, onion powder, pepper, and salt.
4. Pour egg mixture over broccoli and bell pepper and cook for 10 minutes more.
5. Serve and enjoy.

Per serving: Calories: 150kcal; Fat: 9.7g; Carbs: 5.3g; Protein: 11.2g

6. Gruyere Cheese Egg Bite

Preparation time: 10 minutes
Cooking time: 5 minutes
Servings: 7
Ingredients:

- 4 eggs
- 1/4 cup bacon, cooked and crumbled
- 1/2 cup cottage cheese, crumbled
- 1/2 cup gruyere cheese, shredded

Directions:

1. Spray egg mold with cooking spray and set aside.
2. In a bowl, beat eggs until frothy. Add remaining ingredients into the eggs and stir to mix.
3. Pour egg mixture into the prepared egg mold.
4. Place egg mold into the air fryer basket then cook at 330 F for 5 minutes.
5. Serve and enjoy.

Per serving: Calories: 86kcal; Fat: 5.6g; Carbs: 0.8g; Protein: 7.9g

7. Bacon Cheese Egg Bites

Preparation time: 10 minutes
Cooking time: 13 minutes
Servings: 4
Ingredients:

- 4 eggs
- 1/4 cup cheddar cheese, shredded
- 4 bacon slices, cooked and crumbled
- 1/2 small bell pepper, diced
- 1/2 onion, diced
- 4 tsp coconut milk
- Pepper
- Salt

Directions:

1. Spray four ramekins with cooking spray.
2. Crack 1 egg into each ramekin then adds 1 tsp coconut milk into each one.
3. Top each one off with bacon, bell pepper, onion, and cheese. Season with pepper and salt.
4. Place ramekins into the air fryer basket then cook at 300 F for 10-13 minutes.
5. Serve and enjoy.

Per serving: Calories: 216kcal; Fat: 15.9g; Carbs: 3.4g; Protein: 14.8g

8. Cheese Omelet

Preparation time: 10 minutes
Cooking time: 8 minutes
Servings: 2
Ingredients:

- 2 eggs
- 1/4 cup cheddar cheese, shredded
- 1/4 cup heavy cream
- Pepper
- Salt

Directions:

1. Spray air fryer safe pan with cooking spray and set aside.
2. In a bowl, whisk eggs with cream, pepper, and salt.
3. Pour egg mixture into the prepared pan. Place pan in the air fryer basket then cook at 350 F for 4 minutes.
4. Sprinkle cheese on top and cook for 4 minutes more.
5. Serve and enjoy.

Per serving: Calories: 172kcal; Fat: 14.6g; Carbs: 1g; Protein: 9.4g

9. Cheese Sausage Pepper Frittata

Preparation time: 10 minutes
Cooking time: 20 minutes
Servings: 2
Ingredients:

- 4 eggs, lightly beaten
- 1 green onion, chopped
- 2 tbsp bell pepper, diced
- 1/2 cup Monterey jack cheese
- 1/4 lb breakfast sausage, cooked and crumbled
- Pepper
- Salt

Directions:

1. Preheat the cosori air fryer to 360 F.
2. Spray air fryer pan with cooking spray and set aside.
3. In a bowl, whisk eggs with remaining ingredients. Pour egg mixture into the prepared pan.
4. Place pan in the air fryer basket then cook for 18-20 minutes.
5. Serve and enjoy.

Per serving: Calories: 411kcal; Fat: 29.6g; Carbs: 10.7g; Protein: 26.8g

10. Cheese Ham Egg Cups

Preparation time: 10 minutes
Cooking time: 5 minutes
Servings: 4
Ingredients:

- 4 eggs
- 1/2 cup cheddar cheese, shredded
- 4 tbsp heavy cream
- 1/2 cup ham, diced
- Pepper
- Salt

Directions:

1. Spray four ramekins with cooking spray then set aside.
2. In a small bowl, whisk eggs with cheese, heavy cream, ham, pepper, and salt.
3. Pour egg mixture into the prepared ramekins.
4. Place ramekins into the air fryer basket then cook at 300 F for 5 minutes.
5. Serve and enjoy.

Per serving: Calories: 199kcal; Fat: 16.1g; Carbs: 1.6g; Protein: 12.2g

11. Healthy Spinach Omelet

Preparation time: 10 minutes
Cooking time: 8 minutes
Servings: 2
Ingredients:

- 3 eggs
- 1/2 cup cheddar cheese, shredded
- 2 tbsp spinach, chopped
- Pepper
- Salt

Directions:

1. Spray air fryer safe pan with cooking spray and set aside.
2. In a bowl, whisk eggs with cheese, spinach, pepper, and salt.
3. Pour egg mixture into the prepared pan.
4. Place pan into the air fryer basket then cook at 390 F for 8 minutes.
5. Serve and enjoy.

Per serving: Calories: 209kcal; Fat: 15.9g; Carbs: 1g; Protein: 15.4g

12. Breakfast Radish Hash Browns

Preparation time: 10 minutes
Cooking time: 13 minutes
Servings: 2
Ingredients:

- 1 lb radishes, clean and sliced
- 1 onion, sliced
- 1 tbsp olive oil
- 1 tsp onion powder
- 1 tsp garlic powder
- 1/2 tsp paprika
- 1/4 tsp pepper
- 1/2 tsp salt

Directions:

1. Toss sliced radishes and onion with olive oil.
2. Spray air fryer basket with cooking spray.
3. Spray radish and onion mixture into the air fryer basket then cook at 360 F for 8 minutes.
4. Transfer radish and onion mixture into the mixing bowl. Add onion powder, garlic powder, paprika, pepper, and salt and toss well.
5. Return radish and onion mixture into the air fryer basket then cook for 5 minutes more.
6. Serve and enjoy.

Per serving: Calories: 125kcal; Fat: 7.4g; Carbs: 13.6g; Protein: 3.6g

13. Classic Sweet Potato Hash

Preparation time: 10 minutes
Cooking time: 12 minutes
Servings: 4
Ingredients:
- 2 cups sweet potatoes, peeled and diced
- 1 tsp Italian seasoning
- 1 tsp paprika
- 3 tbsp olive oil
- 3 bacon slices, diced
- Pepper
- Salt

Directions:
1. In a mixing bowl, toss sweet potatoes with Italian seasoning, paprika, oil, bacon, pepper, and salt.
2. Add sweet potatoes into the air fryer basket then cook at 400 F for 12 minutes. Shake basket halfway through.
3. Serve and enjoy.

Per serving: Calories: 141kcal; Fat: 9.9g; Carbs: 7.3g; Protein: 5.9g

14. Mushroom Frittata

Preparation time: 10 minutes
Cooking time: 6 minutes
Servings: 2
Ingredients:
- 3 eggs
- 2 tbsp parmesan cheese, shredded
- 2 tbsp cream
- 2 cremini mushrooms, sliced
- 1/4 small onion, chopped
- 1/4 bell pepper, diced
- Pepper
- Salt

Directions:
1. Spray air fryer pan with cooking spray and set aside.
2. Preheat the cosori air fryer to 400 F.
3. In a bowl, whisk eggs with cream, mushrooms, onion, bell pepper, pepper, and salt.
4. Pour egg mixture into the prepared pan.
5. Place pan in the air fryer basket then cook for 5 minutes. Top with cheese and cook for 1 minute more.
6. Serve and enjoy.

Per serving: Calories: 159kcal; Fat: 10.3g; Carbs: 3.9g; Protein: 13.5g

15. Breakfast Cream Souffle

Preparation time: 10 minutes
Cooking time: 10 minutes
Servings: 4
Ingredients:
- 4 eggs
- 1/4 tsp red chili pepper
- 4 tbsp cream
- Pepper
- Salt

Directions:
1. Preheat the cosori air fryer to 390 F.
2. Spray four ramekins with cooking spray then set aside.
3. In a bowl, whisk eggs with red chili pepper, cream, pepper, and salt.
4. Pour egg mixture into the prepared ramekins.
5. Place ramekins into the air fryer basket then cook for 10 minutes.
6. Serve and enjoy.

Per serving: Calories: 71kcal; Fat: 5g; Carbs: 0.8g; Protein: 5.7g

16. Cheese Mushroom Egg Bake

Preparation time: 10 minutes
Cooking time: 8 minutes
Servings: 1
Ingredients:

- 2 eggs
- 1/2 cup ham, diced
- 1/4 cup cheddar cheese, shredded
- 1/4 cup coconut milk
- 2 mushrooms, sliced
- 1 tbsp green onion, chopped
- Pepper
- Salt

Directions:

1. Spray air fryer safe pan with cooking spray and set aside.
2. In a bowl, whisk eggs with cheese, milk, pepper, and salt. Add ham, mushrooms, and green onion and stir well.
3. Pour egg mixture into the prepared pan.
4. Place pan into the air fryer basket then cook at 330 F for 8 minutes.
5. Serve and enjoy.

Per serving: Calories: 498kcal; Fat: 38.3g; Carbs: 8.6g; Protein: 31.9g

17. Spinach Tomato Frittata

Preparation time: 10 minutes
Cooking time: 7 minutes
Servings: 2
Ingredients:

- 2 eggs
- 1/4 cup fresh spinach, chopped
- 1/4 cup tomatoes, chopped
- 2 tbsp cream
- 1 tbsp cheddar cheese, grated
- Pepper
- Salt

Directions:

1. Spray air fryer pan with cooking spray and set aside.
2. In a bowl, whisk eggs with remaining ingredients.
3. Pour egg mixture into the prepared pan. Place pan in the air fryer basket then cook at 330 F for 7 minutes.
4. Serve and enjoy.

Per serving: Calories: 90kcal; Fat: 6.3g; Carbs: 1.8g; Protein: 16.8g

18. Easy Cheesy Breakfast Eggs

Preparation time: 10 minutes
Cooking time: 5 minutes
Servings: 1
Ingredients:

- 2 eggs
- 1 tsp parmesan cheese, grated
- 2 tbsp cheddar cheese, shredded
- 2 tbsp heavy cream
- Pepper
- Salt

Directions:

1. Spray ramekin dish with cooking spray and set aside.
2. In a small bowl, whisk eggs with parmesan cheese, cheddar cheese, heavy cream, pepper, and salt.
3. Pour egg mixture into the prepared ramekin dish.
4. Place ramekin dish into the air fryer basket then cook at 330 F for 5 minutes.
5. Serve and enjoy.

Per serving: Calories: 332kcal; Fat: 27.5g; Carbs: 2.3g; Protein: 19.7g

19. Cheesy Chicken Fritters

Preparation time: 10 minutes
Cooking time: 25 minutes
Servings: 4
Ingredients:

- 1 lb ground chicken
- 3/4 cup almond flour
- 1 egg, lightly beaten
- 1 garlic clove, minced
- 1 1/2 cup mozzarella cheese, shredded
- 1/2 cup shallots, chopped
- 2 cups broccoli, chopped
- Pepper
- Salt

Directions:

1. Line air fryer basket with parchment paper.
2. Add all ingredients into the mixing bowl and mix until well combined.
3. Make patties from mixture and place into the air fryer basket.
4. Cook at 390 F for 15 minutes. Turn patties and cook for 10 minutes more.
5. Serve and enjoy.

Per serving: Calories: 322kcal; Fat: 14.2g; Carbs: 8.2g; Protein: 40.1g

20. Ham Egg Bites

Preparation time: 10 minutes
Cooking time: 12 minutes
Servings: 8
Ingredients:

- 6 eggs
- 1/2 cup cheddar cheese, shredded
- 1 cup ham, diced
- 2 tbsp cream
- 1/4 tsp garlic powder
- 1/4 tsp onion powder
- Pepper
- Salt

Directions:

1. In a bowl, whisk eggs with remaining ingredients.
2. Pour egg mixture into the silicone muffin molds.
3. Place molds into the air fryer basket then cook at 300 F for 12-14 minutes or until eggs are cooked.
4. Serve and enjoy.

Per serving: Calories: 106kcal; Fat: 7.2g; Carbs: 1.2g; Protein: 8.8g

21. Delicious Chicken Burger Patties

Preparation time: 10 minutes
Cooking time: 25 minutes
Servings: 5
Ingredients:

- 1 lb ground chicken
- 1 egg, lightly beaten
- 1 cup Monterey jack cheese, grated
- 1 cup carrot, grated
- 1 cup cauliflower, grated
- 1/8 tsp red pepper flakes
- 2 garlic cloves, minced
- 1/2 cup onion, minced
- 3/4 cup almond flour
- Pepper
- Salt

Directions:

1. Line air fryer basket with parchment paper.
2. Add all ingredients into the mixing bowl and mix until well combined.
3. Make patties from mixture and place into the air fryer basket.
4. Cook at 400 F for 25 minutes. Turn patties halfway through.
5. Serve and enjoy.

Per serving: Calories: 314kcal; Fat: 16.6g; Carbs: 5.9g; Protein: 34.6g

22. Cheese Egg Frittata

Preparation time: 10 minutes
Cooking time: 6 minutes
Servings: 2
Ingredients:

- 4 eggs
- 1/3 cup cheddar cheese, shredded
- 1/2 cup half and half
- Pepper
- Salt

Directions:

1. Spray air fryer safe pan with cooking spray and set aside.
2. In a small bowl, whisk eggs with cheese, half and half, pepper, and salt.
3. Pour egg mixture into the prepared pan.
4. Place pan in the air fryer basket then cook at 320 F for 6 minutes.
5. Serve and enjoy.

Per serving: Calories: 281kcal; Fat: 22g; Carbs: 3.6g; Protein: 17.6g

23. Breakfast Avocado Eggs

Preparation time: 10 minutes
Cooking time: 9 minutes
Servings: 2
Ingredients:

- 2 eggs
- 1 avocado, cut in half and remove the seed
- Pinch of red pepper flakes
- Pepper
- Salt

Directions:

1. Break one egg into each avocado half. Season with red pepper flakes, pepper, and salt.
2. Place avocado halves into the air fryer basket then cook at 400 F for 5 minutes or until eggs are cooked. Check after 5 minutes.
3. Serve and enjoy.

Per serving: Calories: 268kcal; Fat: 24g; Carbs: 9.1g; Protein: 7.5g

24. Basil Feta Egg Bite

Preparation time: 10 minutes
Cooking time: 5 minutes
Servings: 7
Ingredients:

- 4 eggs
- 1 tbsp fresh basil, chopped
- 1/4 cup sun-dried tomatoes, diced
- 1/4 cup feta cheese, crumbled
- 1/2 cup cottage cheese, crumbled

Directions:

1. Spray egg mold with cooking spray and set aside.
2. In a bowl, beat eggs until frothy. Add remaining ingredients into the eggs and stir to mix.
3. Pour egg mixture into the prepared egg mold.
4. Place egg mold into the air fryer basket then cook at 330 F for 5 minutes.
5. Serve and enjoy.

Per serving: Calories: 66kcal; Fat: 4g; Carbs: 1.3g; Protein: 6.2g

25. Sausage Swiss Cheese Egg Bite

Preparation time: 10 minutes
Cooking time: 5 minutes
Servings: 7
Ingredients:

- 4 eggs
- 1 tbsp green onion, chopped
- 1/4 cup mushrooms, chopped
- 1/4 cup sausage, cooked and crumbled

- 1/2 cup cottage cheese, crumbled
- 1/2 cup Swiss cheese, shredded
- Pepper
- Salt

Directions:
1. Spray egg mold with cooking spray and set aside.
2. In a bowl, beat eggs until frothy. Add remaining ingredients into the eggs and stir to mix.
3. Pour egg mixture into the prepared egg mold.
4. Place egg mold into the air fryer basket then cook at 330 F for 5 minutes.
5. Serve and enjoy.

Per serving: Calories: 82kcal; Fat: 5.1g; Carbs: 1.3g; Protein: 7.7g

CHAPTER 2: Vegetable Recipes

26. Curried Eggplant Slices

Preparation time: 10 minutes
Cooking time: 10 minutes
Servings: 4
Ingredients:

- 1 large eggplant, cut into 1/2-inch slices
- 1 garlic clove, minced
- 1 tbsp olive oil
- 1/2 tsp curry powder
- 1/8 tsp turmeric
- Salt

Directions:

1. Preheat the cosori air fryer to 300 F.
2. In a small bowl, mix together oil, garlic, curry powder, turmeric, and salt and rub all over eggplant slices.
3. Add eggplant slices into the air fryer basket then cook for 10 minutes or until lightly browned.
4. Serve and enjoy.

Per serving: Calories: 61kcal; Fat: 3.8g; Carbs: 7.2g; Protein: 1.2g

27. Balsamic Brussels Sprouts

Preparation time: 10 minutes
Cooking time: 10 minutes
Servings: 5
Ingredients:

- 2 cups Brussels sprouts, cut in half
- 1 tbsp olive oil
- 1 tbsp balsamic vinegar
- 1/2 cup onion, sliced
- Pepper
- Salt

Directions:

1. Add brussels sprouts, oil, vinegar, onion, pepper, and salt into the mixing bowl and toss well.
2. Add brussels sprouts mixture into the air fryer basket then cook at 350 F for 5 minutes.
3. Shake basket well and cook for 5 minutes more.
4. Serve and enjoy.

Per serving: Calories: 44kcal; Fat: 2.9g; Carbs: 4.3g; Protein: 1.3g

28. Simple Vegan Broccoli

Preparation time: 10 minutes
Cooking time: 5 minutes
Servings: 2
Ingredients:

- 4 cups broccoli florets
- 1 tbsp nutritional yeast
- 2 tbsp olive oil
- Pepper
- Salt

Directions:

1. In a medium bowl, mix together broccoli, nutritional yeast, oil, pepper, and salt.
2. Add broccoli florets into the air fryer basket then cook at 370 F for 5 minutes.
3. Serve and enjoy.

Per serving: Calories: 158kcal; Fat: 14.3g; Carbs: 6.3g; Protein: 4.3g

29. Easy & Crisp Brussels Sprouts

Preparation time: 10 minutes
Cooking time: 15 minutes
Servings: 4
Ingredients:

- 2 cups Brussels sprouts
- 2 tbsp everything bagel seasoning
- 1/4 cup almonds, crushed
- 1/4 cup parmesan cheese, grated
- 2 tbsp olive oil

- Salt

Directions:
1. Add Brussels sprouts into the saucepan with 2 cups of water. Cover and cook for 8-10 minutes.
2. Drain well and allow to cool completely. Sliced each Brussels sprouts in half.
3. Add Brussels sprouts and remaining ingredients into the mixing bowl and toss to coat.
4. Add Brussels sprouts mixture into the air fryer basket then cook at 375 F for 12-15 minutes.
5. Serve and enjoy.

Per serving: Calories: 144kcal; Fat: 11.5g; Carbs: 7.6g; Protein: 5.1g

30. Asparagus with Almonds

Preparation time: 10 minutes
Cooking time: 5 minutes
Servings: 4
Ingredients:

- 12 asparagus spears
- 1/3 cup sliced almonds
- 2 tbsp olive oil
- 2 tbsp balsamic vinegar
- Pepper
- Salt

Directions:
1. Drizzle asparagus spears with oil and vinegar.
2. Arrange asparagus spears into the air fryer basket and season with pepper and salt.
3. Sprinkle sliced almond over asparagus spears.
4. Cook asparagus at 350 F for 5 minutes. Shake basket halfway through.
5. Serve and enjoy.

Per serving: Calories: 122kcal; Fat: 11.1g; Carbs: 4.6g; Protein: 3.3g

31. Garlicky Cauliflower Florets

Preparation time: 10 minutes
Cooking time: 20 minutes
Servings: 4
Ingredients:

- 5 cups cauliflower florets
- 1/2 tsp cumin powder
- 1/2 tsp ground coriander
- 6 garlic cloves, chopped
- 4 tablespoons olive oil
- 1/2 tsp salt

Directions:
1. Add cauliflower florets and remaining ingredients into the large mixing bowl and toss well.
2. Add cauliflower florets into the air fryer basket then cook at 400 F for 20 minutes. Shake basket halfway through.
3. Serve and enjoy.

Per serving: Calories: 159kcal; Fat: 14.2g; Carbs: 8.2g; Protein: 2.8g

32. Air Fryer Basil Tomatoes

Preparation time: 10 minutes
Cooking time: 25 minutes
Servings: 4
Ingredients:

- 4 large tomatoes, halved
- 1 garlic clove, minced
- 1 tbsp vinegar
- 1 tbsp olive oil
- 2 tbsp parmesan cheese, grated
- 1/2 tsp fresh parsley, chopped
- 1 tsp fresh basil, minced
- Pepper
- Salt

Directions:
1. Preheat the cosori air fryer to 320 F.

2. In a bowl, mix together oil, basil, garlic, vinegar, pepper, and salt. Add tomatoes and stir to coat.
3. Place tomato halves into the air fryer basket then cook for 20 minutes.
4. Sprinkle parmesan cheese over tomatoes and cook for 5 minutes more.
5. Serve and enjoy.

Per serving: Calories: 87kcal; Fat: 5.4g; Carbs: 7.7g; Protein: 3.9g

33. Easy Roasted Vegetables

Preparation time: 10 minutes
Cooking time: 18 minutes
Servings: 6
Ingredients:

- 1/2 cup mushrooms, sliced
- 1/2 cup zucchini, sliced
- 1/2 cup yellow squash, sliced
- 1/2 cup baby carrots
- 1 cup cauliflower florets
- 1 cup broccoli florets
- 1/4 cup parmesan cheese, grated
- 1 tsp red pepper flakes
- 1 tbsp garlic, minced
- 1 tbsp olive oil
- 1/4 cup balsamic vinegar
- 1 small onion, sliced
- 1 tsp sea salt

Directions:
1. Preheat the cosori air fryer to 400 F.
2. In a large mixing bowl, mix together olive oil, garlic, vinegar, red pepper flakes, pepper, and salt.
3. Add vegetables and toss until well coated.
4. Add vegetables into the air fryer basket then cook for 8 minutes. Shake basket then cook for 8 minutes more.
5. Add parmesan cheese and cook for 2 minutes more.
6. Serve and enjoy.

Per serving: Calories: 59kcal; Fat: 3.4g; Carbs: 5.3g; Protein: 2.8g

34. Easy Roasted Carrots

Preparation time: 10 minutes
Cooking time: 18 minutes
Servings: 4
Ingredients:

- 16 oz carrots, peeled and cut into 2-inch chunks
- 1 tsp olive oil
- Pepper
- Salt

Directions:
1. Preheat the cosori air fryer to 360 F.
2. Toss carrots with oil and season with pepper and salt.
3. Add carrots into the air fryer basket then cook for 15-18 minutes. Shake basket 3-4 times.
4. Serve and enjoy.

Per serving: Calories: 57kcal; Fat: 1.2g; Carbs: 11.2g; Protein: 0.9g

35. Curried Cauliflower with Pine Nuts

Preparation time: 10 minutes
Cooking time: 10 minutes
Servings: 4
Ingredients:

- 1 small cauliflower head, cut into florets
- 2 tbsp olive oil
- 1/4 cup pine nuts, toasted
- 1 tbsp curry powder
- 1/4 tsp salt

Directions:
1. Preheat the cosori air fryer to 350 F.
2. In a mixing bowl, toss cauliflower florets with oil, curry powder, and salt.

3. Add cauliflower florets into the air fryer basket then cook for 10 minutes. Shake basket halfway through.
4. Transfer cauliflower into the serving bowl. Add pine nuts and toss well.
5. Serve and enjoy.

Per serving: Calories: 139kcal; Fat: 13.1g; Carbs: 5.5g; Protein: 2.7g

36. Spiced Green Beans

Preparation time: 10 minutes
Cooking time: 10 minutes
Servings: 2
Ingredients:

- 2 cups green beans
- 1/8 tsp ground allspice
- 1/4 tsp ground cinnamon
- 1/2 tsp dried oregano
- 2 tbsp olive oil
- 1/4 tsp ground coriander
- 1/4 tsp ground cumin
- 1/8 tsp cayenne pepper
- 1/2 tsp salt

Directions:
1. Add all ingredients into the medium bowl and toss well.
2. Spray air fryer basket with cooking spray.
3. Add green beans into the air fryer basket then cook at 370 F for 10 minutes. Shake basket halfway through
4. Serve and enjoy.

Per serving: Calories: 158kcal; Fat: 14.3g; Carbs: 8.6g; Protein: 2.1g

37. Parmesan Brussels sprouts

Preparation time: 10 minutes
Cooking time: 12 minutes
Servings: 4
Ingredients:

- 1 lb Brussels sprouts, remove stems and halved
- 1/4 cup parmesan cheese, grated
- 2 tbsp olive oil
- Pepper
- Salt

Directions:
1. Preheat the cosori air fryer to 350 F.
2. In a mixing bowl, toss Brussels sprouts with oil, pepper, and salt.
3. Transfer Brussels sprouts into the air fryer basket then cook for 12 minutes. Shake basket halfway through.
4. Sprinkle with parmesan cheese and serve.

Per serving: Calories: 129kcal; Fat: 8.7g; Carbs: 10.6g; Protein: 5.9g

38. Air Fryer Ratatouille

Preparation time: 10 minutes
Cooking time: 15 minutes
Servings: 6
Ingredients:

- 1 eggplant, diced
- 1 onion, diced
- 3 tomatoes, diced
- 1 red bell pepper, diced
- 1 green bell pepper, diced
- 1 tbsp vinegar
- 2 tbsp olive oil
- 2 tbsp herb de Provence
- 2 garlic cloves, chopped
- Pepper
- Salt

Directions:
1. Preheat the cosori air fryer to 400 F.
2. Add all ingredients into the bowl and toss well and transfer into the air fryer safe dish.

3. Place dish into the air fryer basket then cook for 15 minutes. Stir halfway through.
4. Serve and enjoy.

Per serving: Calories: 91kcal; Fat: 5g; Carbs: 11.6g; Protein: 1.9g

39. Flavorful Tomatoes

Preparation time: 10 minutes
Cooking time: 15 minutes
Servings: 4
Ingredients:

- 4 Roma tomatoes, sliced, remove seeds pithy portion
- 1 tbsp olive oil
- 1/2 tsp dried thyme
- 2 garlic cloves, minced
- Pepper
- Salt

Directions:
1. Preheat the cosori air fryer to 390 F.
2. Toss sliced tomatoes with oil, thyme, garlic, pepper, and salt.
3. Arrange sliced tomatoes into the air fryer basket then cook for 15 minutes.
4. Serve and enjoy.

Per serving: Calories: 55kcal; Fat: 3.8g; Carbs: 5.4g; Protein: 1.2g

40. Healthy Mixed Vegetables

Preparation time: 10 minutes
Cooking time: 10 minutes
Servings: 6
Ingredients:

- 2 cups mushrooms, cut in half
- 2 yellow squash, sliced
- 2 medium zucchinis, sliced
- 3/4 tsp Italian seasoning
- 1/2 onion, sliced
- 1/2 cup olive oil
- 1/2 tsp garlic salt

Directions:
1. Add vegetables and remaining ingredients into the mixing bowl and toss well.
2. Add vegetables into the air fryer basket then cook at 400 F for 10 minutes. Shake basket halfway through.
3. Serve and enjoy.

Per serving: Calories: 176kcal; Fat: 17.3g; Carbs: 6.2g; Protein: 2.5g

41. Healthy Roasted Carrots

Preparation time: 10 minutes
Cooking time: 12 minutes
Servings: 4
Ingredients:

- 2 cups carrots, peeled and chopped
- 1 tsp cumin
- 1 tbsp olive oil
- 1/4 fresh coriander, chopped

Directions:
1. Toss carrots with cumin and oil and place them into the air fryer basket.
2. Cook at 390 F for 12 minutes.
3. Garnish with fresh coriander and serve.

Per serving: Calories: 55kcal; Fat: 3.6g; Carbs: 5.7g; Protein: 0.6g

42. Healthy Squash & Zucchini

Preparation time: 10 minutes
Cooking time: 25 minutes
Servings: 4
Ingredients:

- 1 lb zucchini, cut into 1/2-inch half-moons
- 1 lb yellow squash, cut into 1/2-inch half-moons
- 1 tbsp olive oil
- Pepper
- Salt

Directions:

1. In a mixing bowl, add zucchini, squash, oil, pepper, and salt and toss well.
2. Add zucchini and squash mixture into the air fryer basket then cook at 400 F for 20 minutes. Shake basket halfway through.
3. Shake basket well and cook for 5 minutes more.
4. Serve and enjoy.

Per serving: Calories: 66kcal; Fat: 3.9g; Carbs: 7.6g; Protein: 2.7g

43. Garlic Green Beans

Preparation time: 10 minutes
Cooking time: 8 minutes
Servings: 4
Ingredients:

- 1 lb fresh green beans, trimmed
- 1 tsp garlic powder
- 1 tbsp olive oil
- Pepper
- Salt

Directions:

1. Drizzle green beans with oil and season with garlic powder, pepper, and salt.
2. Place green beans into the air fryer basket then cook at 370 F for 8 minutes. Toss halfway through.
3. Serve and enjoy.

Per serving: Calories: 68kcal; Fat: 3.7g; Carbs: 8.6g; Protein: 2.2g

44. Asian Broccoli

Preparation time: 10 minutes
Cooking time: 20 minutes
Servings: 4
Ingredients:

- 1 lb broccoli florets
- 1 tsp rice vinegar
- 2 tsp sriracha
- 2 tbsp soy sauce
- 1 tbsp garlic, minced
- 1 1/2 tbsp sesame oil
- Salt

Directions:

1. Toss broccoli florets with garlic, sesame oil, and salt.
2. Add broccoli florets into the air fryer basket then cook at 400 F for 15-20 minutes. Shake basket halfway through.
3. In a mixing bowl, mix together rice vinegar, sriracha, and soy sauce. Add broccoli and toss well.
4. Serve and enjoy.

Per serving: Calories: 94kcal; Fat: 5.5g; Carbs: 9.3g; Protein: 3.8g

45. Crunchy Fried Cabbage

Preparation time: 10 minutes
Cooking time: 10 minutes
Servings: 2
Ingredients:

- 1/2 cabbage head, sliced into 2-inch slices
- 1 tbsp olive oil
- Pepper
- Salt

Directions:

1. Drizzle cabbage with olive oil then season with pepper and salt.
2. Add cabbage slices into the air fryer basket then cook at 375 F for 5 minutes.
3. Toss cabbage well and cook for 5 minutes more.
4. Serve and enjoy.

Per serving: Calories: 105kcal; Fat: 7.2g; Carbs: 10.4g; Protein: 2.3g

CHAPTER 3: Chicken and Poultry

46. Perfect Chicken Thighs Dinner

Preparation time: 10 minutes
Cooking time: 15 minutes
Servings: 4
Ingredients:

- 4 chicken thighs, bone-in & skinless
- 1/4 tsp ground ginger
- 2 tsp paprika
- 2 tsp garlic powder
- 1/4 tsp pepper
- 1 tsp salt

Directions:

1. Preheat the cosori air fryer to 400 F.
2. In a small bowl, mix together ginger, paprika, garlic powder, pepper, and salt and rub all over chicken thighs.
3. Spray chicken thighs with cooking spray.
4. Place chicken thighs into the air fryer basket then cook for 10 minutes.
5. Turn chicken thighs and cook for 5 minutes more.
6. Serve and enjoy.

Per serving: Calories: 286kcal; Fat: 11g; Carbs: 1.8g; Protein: 42.7g

47. Flavors Dijon Chicken

Preparation time: 10 minutes
Cooking time: 14 minutes
Servings: 6
Ingredients:

- 1 1/2 lbs chicken breasts, boneless
- 1/4 tsp cayenne
- 1 tsp Italian seasoning
- 1 tbsp coconut aminos
- 1 tbsp fresh lemon juice
- 1 tbsp Dijon mustard
- 1/2 cup mayonnaise
- 1/2 tsp pepper
- 1 tsp sea salt

Directions:

1. In a small bowl, mix together mayonnaise, cayenne, Italian seasoning, coconut amino, lemon juice, mustard, pepper, and salt.
2. Add chicken into the zip-lock bag. Pour mayonnaise mixture over chicken and mix well.
3. Seal Ziplock bag and place in the refrigerator overnight.
4. Preheat the cosori air fryer to 400 F.
5. Place marinated chicken in the air fryer basket then cook for 14 minutes. Turn chicken halfway through.
6. Serve and enjoy.

Per serving: Calories: 300kcal; Fat: 15.3g; Carbs: 5.6g; Protein: 33.2g

48. Nutritious Chicken & Veggies

Preparation time: 10 minutes
Cooking time: 10 minutes
Servings: 4
Ingredients:

- 1 lb chicken breast, boneless & cut into bite-size pieces
- 1 tbsp Italian seasoning
- 1/2 tsp garlic powder
- 1/2 tsp chili powder
- 2 tbsp olive oil
- 2 garlic cloves, minced
- 1/2 onion, chopped
- 1 cup bell pepper, chopped
- 1 zucchini, chopped
- 1 cup broccoli florets
- Pepper

- Salt

Directions:
1. Preheat the cosori air fryer to 400 F.
2. Add chicken and remaining ingredients into the large mixing bowl and toss well.
3. Add chicken and veggies mixture into the air fryer basket then cook for 10 minutes or until chicken is cooked. Shake air fryer basket halfway through.
4. Serve and enjoy.

Per serving: Calories: 235kcal; Fat: 11.2g; Carbs: 8g; Protein: 25.9g

49. Turkey Spinach Patties

Preparation time: 10 minutes
Cooking time: 20 minutes
Servings: 4
Ingredients:

- 1 lb ground turkey
- 1 1/2 cups fresh spinach, chopped
- 1 tsp Italian seasoning
- 1 tbsp olive oil
- 1 tbsp garlic, minced
- 4 oz feta cheese, crumbled
- Pepper
- Salt

Directions:
1. Add ground turkey and remaining ingredients into the mixing bowl and mix until well combined.
2. Make four equal shapes of patties from turkey mixture and place it into the air fryer basket.
3. Cook turkey patties for 20 minutes.
4. Serve and enjoy.

Per serving: Calories: 336kcal; Fat: 22.4g; Carbs: 2.4g; Protein: 35.5g

50. Perfectly Spiced Chicken Tenders

Preparation time: 10 minutes
Cooking time: 13 minutes
Servings: 4
Ingredients:

- 6 chicken tenders
- 1 tsp onion powder
- 1 tsp oregano
- 1 tsp garlic powder
- 1 tsp paprika
- 1 tsp kosher salt

Directions:
1. Preheat the cosori air fryer to 380 F.
2. In a small bowl, mix together onion powder, oregano, garlic powder, paprika, and salt and rub all over chicken tenders.
3. Spray chicken tenders with cooking spray.
4. Bring chicken tenders into the air fryer basket then cook for 13 minutes.
5. Serve and enjoy.

Per serving: Calories: 423kcal; Fat: 16.4g; Carbs: 1.5g; Protein: 63.7g

51. Perfect Chicken Breasts

Preparation time: 10 minutes
Cooking time: 15 minutes
Servings: 4
Ingredients:

- 1 lb chicken breasts, skinless and boneless
- 1 tsp poultry seasoning
- 2 tsp olive oil
- 1 tsp salt

Directions:
1. Rub chicken breasts with oil and season with poultry seasoning and salt.

2. Place chicken breasts into the air fryer basket then cook at 360 F for 10 minutes. Flip chicken and cook for 5 minutes more.
3. Serve and enjoy.

Per serving: Calories: 237kcal; Fat: 10.8g; Carbs: 0.3g; Protein: 32.9g

52. Tasty Turkey Fajitas

Preparation time: 10 minutes
Cooking time: 20 minutes
Servings: 4
Ingredients:

- 1 lb turkey breast, boneless, skinless, and cut into 1/2-inch slices
- 1/4 cup fresh cilantro, chopped
- 1 jalapeno pepper, chopped
- 1 onion, sliced
- 2 bell pepper, sliced into strips
- 1 1/2 tbsp olive oil
- 2 lime juice
- 1/2 tsp onion powder
- 1 tsp garlic powder
- 1/2 tbsp oregano
- 1/2 tsp paprika
- 1 tbsp chili powder

Directions:

1. In a small bowl, mix together onion powder, garlic powder, oregano, paprika, cumin, chili powder, and pepper.
2. Squeeze one lime juice over turkey breast then sprinkle spice mixture over turkey breast.
3. Brush turkey breast with 1 tbsp olive oil and set aside.
4. Add onion and bell peppers into the medium bowl and toss with remaining oil.
5. Preheat the cosori air fryer to 375 F.
6. Add onion and bell peppers into the air fryer basket then cook for 8 minutes. Shake basket then cook for 5 minutes more.
7. Add jalapenos and cook for 5 minutes. Shake basket and add sliced turkey over vegetables and cook for 8 minutes.
8. Garnish fajitas with cilantro and serve.

Per serving: Calories: 211kcal; Fat: 7.8g; Carbs: 16.2g; Protein: 20.9g

53. Lemon Pepper Turkey Breast

Preparation time: 10 minutes
Cooking time: 60 minutes
Servings: 6
Ingredients:

- 3 lbs turkey breast, de-boned
- 1 tsp lemon pepper seasoning
- 1 tbsp Worcestershire sauce
- 2 tbsp olive oil
- 1/2 tsp salt

Directions:

1. Add olive oil, Worcestershire sauce, lemon pepper seasoning, and salt into the zip-lock bag. Add turkey breast to the marinade and coat well and marinate for 1-2 hours.
2. Remove turkey breast from marinade and place it into the air fryer basket.
3. Cook at 350 F for 25 minutes. Turn turkey breast and cook for 35 minutes more or until the internal temperature of turkey breast reaches 165 F.
4. Slice and serve.

Per serving: Calories: 279kcal; Fat: 8.4g; Carbs: 10.3g; Protein: 38.8g

54. Juicy Chicken Breasts

Preparation time: 10 minutes
Cooking time: 10 minutes
Servings: 4
Ingredients:

- 4 chicken breasts, boneless
- 1/8 tsp cayenne pepper
- 1/2 tsp paprika
- 1/2 tsp dried parsley
- 1/2 tsp onion powder
- 1/2 tsp garlic powder
- Pepper
- Salt

Directions:
1. Add 6 cups warm water and 1/4 cup kosher salt into the large bowl and stir until salt dissolve.
2. Add chicken breasts into the water and place a bowl in the refrigerator for 2 hours to brine.
3. After 2 hours remove water and pat dry chicken breasts with paper towels.
4. In a bowl, mix together garlic powder, onion powder, dried parsley, paprika, cayenne pepper, and pepper.
5. Spray chicken breasts with cooking spray then rub with spice mixture.
6. Preheat the cosori air fryer to 380 F.
7. Place chicken breasts into the air fryer basket then cook for 10 minutes. Turn chicken breasts halfway through.
8. Serve and enjoy.

Per serving: Calories: 281kcal; Fat: 10.9g; Carbs: 0.7g; Protein: 42.4g

55. Healthy Chicken & Broccoli

Preparation time: 10 minutes
Cooking time: 20 minutes
Servings: 4
Ingredients:

- 1/2 onion, sliced
- 1 lb chicken breast, boneless, skinless, and cut into bite-size pieces
- 2 cups broccoli florets
- 2 tsp rice vinegar
- 1 tsp sesame oil
- 1 tbsp soy sauce
- 1 tsp garlic, minced
- 2 tbsp olive oil
- Pepper
- Salt

Directions:
1. In a mixing bowl, mix together olive oil, garlic, soy sauce, sesame oil, rice, vinegar, pepper, and salt.
2. Add chicken, onion, and broccoli into the bowl and mix well and marinate for 1 hour.
3. Place marinated chicken and vegetables into the air fryer basket then cook for 380 F for 20 minutes. Shake air fryer basket 2-3 times.
4. Serve and enjoy.

Per serving: Calories: 217kcal; Fat: 11.1g; Carbs: 3.3g; Protein: 25.1g

56. Tender Turkey Legs

Preparation time: 10 minutes
Cooking time: 27 minutes
Servings: 4
Ingredients:

- 4 turkey legs
- 1/4 tsp thyme
- 1/4 tsp oregano
- 1/4 tsp rosemary
- 1 tbsp butter
- Pepper
- Salt

Directions:
1. Season turkey legs with pepper and salt.
2. In a small bowl, mix together butter, thyme, oregano, and rosemary.
3. Rub the butter mixture all over turkey legs.
4. Preheat the cosori air fryer to 350 F.

5. Bring turkey legs into the air fryer basket then cook for 27 minutes.
6. Serve and enjoy.

Per serving: Calories: 182kcal; Fat: 9.9g; Carbs: 1.9g; Protein: 20.2g

57. Chicken Spinach Meatballs

Preparation time: 10 minutes
Cooking time: 10 minutes
Servings: 4
Ingredients:

- 1 lb ground chicken
- 3/4 cup almond flour
- 1/4 cup feta cheese, crumbled
- 2 tbsp parmesan cheese, grated
- 1/4 cup sun-dried tomatoes, drained
- 2 tsp garlic
- 3 cups baby spinach
- Pepper
- Salt

Directions:

1. Add spinach, sun-dried tomatoes, and 1 tsp garlic into the food processor and process until a paste is formed.
2. Add spinach mixture into the large mixing bowl. Add remaining ingredients into the bowl and mix until well combined.
3. Spray air fryer basket with cooking spray.
4. Make small meatballs from mixture and place into the air fryer basket.
5. Cook meatballs at 400 F for 10 minutes.
6. Serve and enjoy.

Per serving: Calories: 303kcal; Fat: 14.7g; Carbs: 3.5g; Protein: 38.4g

58. Flavorful Chicken Tenders

Preparation time: 10 minutes
Cooking time: 12 minutes
Servings: 4
Ingredients:

- 1 lb chicken tenders
- 1/4 tsp oregano
- 1/4 tsp ground mustard
- 1/4 tsp onion powder
- 1/2 tsp garlic powder
- 1/2 tsp paprika
- 1 cup almond flour
- 2 eggs, lightly beaten
- 1/2 tsp pepper
- 1/2 tsp celery salt
- 1/2 tsp salt

Directions:

1. Preheat the cosori air fryer to 400 F.
2. Add eggs into the shallow bowl and set aside.
3. In a separate shallow bowl, mix together almond flour, oregano, mustard, onion powder, garlic powder, paprika, pepper, celery salt, and salt.
4. Dip chicken tenders into the egg wash then coat with almond flour mixture.
5. Place coated chicken tenders into the air fryer basket. Spray top of chicken tenders with cooking spray.
6. Cook chicken tenders for 12 minutes. Turn halfway through.
7. Serve and enjoy.

Per serving: Calories: 291kcal; Fat: 14.2g; Carbs: 2.5g; Protein: 37.3g

59. Juicy Lemon Pepper Chicken Thighs

Preparation time: 10 minutes
Cooking time: 12 minutes
Servings: 4
Ingredients:

- 6 chicken thighs, boneless and skinless
- 1 tbsp lemon zest
- 1/2 tsp dried oregano
- 1 tsp garlic powder
- 1 tsp paprika
- 2 1/2 tbsp fresh lemon juice
- 1 1/2 tsp pepper
- Salt

Directions:

1. Add chicken thighs into the large mixing bowl.
2. Add oregano, garlic powder, paprika, lemon juice, pepper, and salt over chicken and coat well. Place in refrigerator for 30 minutes.
3. Place marinated chicken thighs into the air fryer basket then cook for 12 minutes. Turn halfway through.
4. Garnish with lemon zest and serve.

Per serving: Calories: 426kcal; Fat: 16.5g; Carbs: 2g; Protein: 63.8g

60. Flavors & Crisp Chicken Thighs

Preparation time: 10 minutes
Cooking time: 22 minutes
Servings: 4
Ingredients:

- 4 chicken thighs, bone-in, skin-on, & remove excess fat
- 3/4 tsp onion powder
- 1/2 tsp oregano
- 3/4 tsp garlic powder
- 1 tsp paprika
- 1 tbsp olive oil
- 1/2 tsp kosher salt

Directions:

1. Preheat the cosori air fryer to 380 F.
2. Add chicken thighs into the large zip-lock bag. Add spices and oil over chicken.
3. Seal zip-lock bag and shake well to coat.
4. Place chicken thighs in the air fryer basket skin side down and cook for 12 minutes.
5. Turn chicken thighs and cook for 10 minutes more.
6. Serve and enjoy.

Per serving: Calories: 313kcal; Fat: 14.3g; Carbs: 1.2g; Protein: 42.5g

61. Creamy Pesto Chicken

Preparation time: 10 minutes
Cooking time: 15 minutes
Servings: 4
Ingredients:

- 1 lb chicken thighs, boneless, skinless, & cut into halves
- 1/2 tsp red pepper flakes
- 1/4 cup parmesan cheese, shredded
- 1/4 cup half and half
- 1/2 cup pesto
- 1/2 cup cherry tomatoes, cut in half
- 1/2 cup bell peppers, sliced
- 1/2 cup onion, sliced

Directions:

1. Spray 6*3 heat-safe pan with cooking spray and set aside.
2. In a mixing bowl, mix together pesto, red pepper flakes, half and half, and parmesan cheese.
3. Add chicken into the pesto mixture and coat well.
4. Pour chicken pesto mixture into the prepared pan and top with tomatoes, bell peppers, and onions.

5. Place pan in the air fryer basket then cook at 360 F for 15 minutes.
6. Serve and enjoy.

Per serving: Calories: 406kcal; Fat: 24.6g; Carbs: 6.4g; Protein: 38.8g

62. Greek Meatballs

Preparation time: 10 minutes
Cooking time: 10 minutes
Servings: 4
Ingredients:

- 1 lb ground chicken
- 1 egg, lightly beaten
- 1 tsp onion powder
- 1 tsp lemon zest
- 1 tbsp dried oregano
- 1 1/2 tsp garlic paste
- Pepper
- Salt

Directions:

1. Add all ingredients into the mixing bowl and mix until well combined.
2. Preheat the cosori air fryer to 390 F.
3. Make small meatballs from mixture and place into the air fryer basket then cook for 8-10 minutes.
4. Serve and enjoy.

Per serving: Calories: 239kcal; Fat: 9.6g; Carbs: 1.8g; Protein: 34.5g

63. Crispy Crusted Chicken Tenders

Preparation time: 10 minutes
Cooking time: 10 minutes
Servings: 6
Ingredients:

- 2 eggs, lightly beaten
- 6 chicken tenders
- 1/2 tsp onion powder
- 1/2 tsp garlic powder
- 1 tsp paprika
- 1 cup pork rinds, crushed
- 1 tsp salt

Directions:

1. In a shallow bowl, mix together crushed pork rinds, paprika, garlic powder, onion powder, and salt.
2. In a different shallow bowl, add beaten eggs.
3. Dip chicken tenders in eggs then coat with crushed pork rind mixture.
4. Place coated chicken tenders in the air fryer basket then cook at 400 F for 10 minutes. Turn chicken tenders halfway through.
5. Serve and enjoy.

Per serving: Calories: 66kcal; Fat: 3.5g; Carbs: 0.6g; Protein: 7.9g

64. Quick & Easy Lemon Pepper Chicken

Preparation time: 10 minutes
Cooking time: 30 minutes
Servings: 4
Ingredients:

- 4 chicken breasts, boneless & skinless
- 1 1/2 tsp granulated garlic
- 1 tbsp lemon pepper seasoning
- 1 tsp salt

Directions:

1. Preheat the cosori air fryer to 360 F.
2. Season chicken breasts with lemon pepper seasoning, granulated garlic, and salt.
3. Place chicken into the air fryer basket then cook for 30 minutes. Turn chicken halfway through.
4. Serve and enjoy.

Per serving: Calories: 285kcal; Fat: 10.9g; Carbs: 1.8g; Protein: 42.6g

65. Tender & Juicy Cornish Hens

Preparation time: 10 minutes
Cooking time: 45 minutes

Servings: 4
Ingredients:
- 2 Cornish game hens
- 1/2 tsp dried thyme
- 1/2 tsp dried oregano
- 1/2 tsp dried basil
- 1 tsp paprika
- 1 tsp garlic powder
- 1 tsp pepper
- 2 tbsp olive oil
- 1 tbsp kosher salt

Directions:
1. In a small bowl, mix together oil, garlic powder, paprika, basil, oregano, thyme, pepper, and salt.
2. Rub oil spice mixture all over hens.
3. Place hens in the air fryer basket breast side down and cook for 35 minutes at 360 F.
4. Turn the hens and cook for 10 minutes more.
5. Serve and enjoy.

Per serving: Calories: 400kcal; Fat: 30.5g; Carbs: 1.4g; Protein: 28.9g

CHAPTER 4: Fish and Seafoods

66. Garlic Yogurt Salmon Fillets

Preparation time: 10 minutes
Cooking time: 15 minutes
Servings: 2
Ingredients:

- 2 salmon fillets
- 1/2 tsp garlic powder
- 1/4 cup Greek yogurt
- 1 tsp fresh lemon juice
- 1 tbsp fresh dill, chopped
- 1 lemon, sliced
- Pepper
- Salt

Directions:

1. Place lemon slices in the bottom of the air fryer basket.
2. Season salmon fillets with pepper and salt and place on a lemon slice in the air fryer basket.
3. Cook salmon fillets at 330 F for 15 minutes.
4. Place cooked salmon fillets on a serving plate.
5. Mix together yogurt, dill, lemon juice, and garlic powder.
6. Pour yogurt mixture overcooked salmon and serve.

Per serving: Calories: 277kcal; Fat: 11.9g; Carbs: 5.6g; Protein: 38.8g

67. Old Bay Shrimp

Preparation time: 10 minutes
Cooking time: 10 minutes
Servings: 4
Ingredients:

- 12 oz shrimp, peeled
- 3.25 oz pork rind, crushed
- 1 1/2 tsp old bay seasoning
- 1/4 cup mayonnaise

Directions:

1. Spray air fryer basket with cooking spray.
2. In a shallow bowl, mix together crushed pork rind and old bay seasoning.
3. Add shrimp and mayonnaise into the mixing bowl and toss well.
4. Coat shrimp with pork rind mixture and place it into the air fryer basket.
5. Cook shrimp at 380 F for 10 minutes.
6. Serve and enjoy.

Per serving: Calories: 290kcal; Fat: 14.6g; Carbs: 4.8g; Protein: 34.3g

68. Lemon Garlic White Fish

Preparation time: 10 minutes
Cooking time: 10 minutes
Servings: 2
Ingredients:

- 12 oz white fish fillets
- 1/2 tsp onion powder
- 1/2 tsp lemon pepper seasoning
- 1/2 tsp garlic powder
- Pepper
- Salt

Directions:

1. Preheat the cosori air fryer to 360 F.
2. Spray fish fillets with cooking spray and season with onion powder, lemon pepper seasoning, garlic powder, pepper, and salt.
3. Bring parchment paper in the bottom of the air fryer basket. Place fish fillets into the air fryer basket then cook for 6-10 minutes.
4. Serve and enjoy.

Per serving: Calories: 298kcal; Fat: 12.8g; Carbs: 1.4g; Protein: 41.9g

69. Juicy & Tender Cod Fillets

Preparation time: 10 minutes
Cooking time: 12 minutes
Servings: 2
Ingredients:

- 1 lb cod fillets
- 1/4 cup butter, melted
- 1 lemon, sliced
- 1 tsp salt

Directions:

1. Brush cod fillets with melted butter and season with salt.
2. Place cod fillets into the air fryer basket and top with sliced lemon.
3. Cook at 400 F for 10-12 minutes or until the internal temperature of fish fillets reaches 145 F.
4. Serve and enjoy.

Per serving: Calories: 394kcal; Fat: 25.1g; Carbs: 2.7g; Protein: 41.1g

70. Healthy Crab Cakes

Preparation time: 10 minutes
Cooking time: 10 minutes
Servings: 4
Ingredients:

- 8 oz lump crab meat
- 2 tbsp butter, melted
- 2 tsp Dijon mustard
- 1 tbsp mayonnaise
- 1 egg, lightly beaten
- 1/2 tsp old bay seasoning
- 1 green onion, sliced
- 2 tbsp parsley, chopped
- 1/4 cup almond flour
- Pepper
- Salt

Directions:

1. Add crab meat, mustard, mayonnaise, egg, old bay seasoning, green onion, parsley, almond flour, pepper, and salt into the mixing bowl and mix until well combined.
2. Make four equal shapes of patties from mixture and place on a waxed paper-lined dish and refrigerate for 30 minutes.
3. Brush melted butter over both sides of patties and place into the air fryer basket.
4. Cook patties at 350 F for 10 minutes. Turn halfway through.
5. Serve and enjoy.

Per serving: Calories: 136kcal; Fat: 13.7g; Carbs: 2.8g; Protein: 10.3g

71. Lime Garlic Shrimp Kababs

Preparation time: 10 minutes
Cooking time: 8 minutes
Servings: 2
Ingredients:

- 1 cup raw shrimp
- 1 lime juice
- 1 garlic cloves, minced
- Pepper
- Salt

Directions:

1. Preheat the cosori air fryer to 350 F.
2. In a mixing bowl, mix together shrimp, lime juice, garlic, pepper, and salt.
3. Thread shrimp onto the skewers and place them into the air fryer basket then cook for 8 minutes. Turn halfway through.
4. Serve and enjoy.

Per serving: Calories: 201kcal; Fat: 2.8g; Carbs: 4.9g; Protein: 37.2g

72. Tasty Chipotle Shrimp

Preparation time: 10 minutes
Cooking time: 8 minutes
Servings: 4
Ingredients:

- 1 1/2 lbs shrimp, peeled & deveined
- 2 tbsp olive oil
- 4 tbsp lime juice
- 1/4 tsp ground cumin
- 2 tsp chipotle in adobo

Directions:

1. Add shrimp, oil, lime juice, cumin, and chipotle in a zip-lock bag. Seal bag shake well and place it in the refrigerator for 30 minutes.
2. Thread marinated shrimp onto skewers and place skewers into the air fryer basket.
3. Cook at 350 F for 8 minutes.
4. Serve and enjoy.

Per serving: Calories: 274kcal; Fat: 10g; Carbs: 6.4g; Protein: 39g

73. Perfectly Tender Frozen Fish Fillets

Preparation time: 10 minutes
Cooking time: 12 minutes
Servings: 4
Ingredients:

- 4 tilapia fish fillets, frozen
- 1 lemon, sliced
- 1/2 tsp onion powder
- 1/2 tsp garlic powder
- 1/2 tsp lemon pepper seasoning
- 1/2 tsp salt

Directions:

1. Spray air fryer basket with cooking spray.
2. Season tilapia fillets with onion powder, garlic powder, lemon pepper seasoning, and salt.
3. Place tilapia fillets into the air fryer basket then top with lemon slices.
4. Cook at 390 F for 12 minutes.
5. Serve and enjoy.

Per serving: Calories: 116kcal; Fat: 2g; Carbs: 2g; Protein: 22.9g

74. Ginger Garlic Salmon

Preparation time: 10 minutes
Cooking time: 10 minutes
Servings: 2
Ingredients:

- 2 salmon fillets, boneless and skinless
- 2 tbsp mirin
- 2 tbsp soy sauce
- 1 tbsp olive oil
- 2 tbsp scallions, minced
- 1 tbsp ginger, grated
- 2 garlic cloves, minced

Directions:

1. Add salmon fillets into the zip-lock bag.
2. In a small bowl, mix together mirin, soy sauce, olive oil, scallions, ginger, and garlic and pour over salmon. Seal bag shake well and place it in the refrigerator for 30 minutes.
3. Place marinated salmon fillets into the air fryer basket then cook at 360 F for 10 minutes.
4. Serve and enjoy.

Per serving: Calories: 345kcal; Fat: 18.2g; Carbs: 11.6g; Protein: 36.1g

75. Flavorful Parmesan Shrimp

Preparation time: 10 minutes
Cooking time: 10 minutes
Servings: 6
Ingredients:

- 2 lbs jumbo shrimp, peeled and deveined
- 2 tbsp olive oil
- 1 tsp onion powder
- 1 tsp basil
- 1/2 tsp oregano
- 2/3 cup parmesan cheese, grated
- 1 tbsp garlic, minced
- Pepper
- Salt

Directions:
1. Spray air fryer basket with cooking spray.
2. In a mixing bowl, mix together parmesan cheese, garlic, oregano, basil, onion powder, oil, pepper, and salt.
3. Add shrimp into the bowl and toss well to coat.
4. Place shrimp into the air fryer basket then cook at 350 F for 10 minutes.
5. Serve and enjoy.

Per serving: Calories: 187kcal; Fat: 7g; Carbs: 1.3g; Protein: 30.6g

76. Crisp Bacon Wrapped Scallops

Preparation time: 10 minutes
Cooking time: 8 minutes
Servings: 4
Ingredients:

- 16 scallops, clean and pat dry with paper towels
- 8 bacon slices, cut each slice in half
- Pepper
- Salt

Directions:
1. Preheat the cosori air fryer to 400 F.
2. Place bacon slices into the air fryer basket then cook for 3 minutes. Turn halfway through.
3. Wrap each scallop in bacon slice and secure with a toothpick. Season with pepper and salt.
4. Spray wrapped scallops with cooking spray and place into the air fryer basket.
5. Cook scallops for 8 minutes. Turn halfway through.
6. Serve and enjoy.

Per serving: Calories: 311kcal; Fat: 16.8g; Carbs: 3.4g; Protein: 34.2g

77. Chili Lime Cod

Preparation time: 10 minutes
Cooking time: 13 minutes
Servings: 2
Ingredients:

- 2 cod fillets
- 1 lime zest
- 1 tbsp olive oil
- 1/8 tsp cayenne pepper
- 1/4 tsp ground cumin
- 1/2 tsp garlic powder
- 1/2 tsp chili powder
- 1/2 tsp dried oregano
- 1 tsp dried parsley
- 1 tsp paprika
- 1/4 tsp pepper

Directions:
1. Line air fryer basket with parchment paper.
2. In a small bowl, mix together cayenne pepper, cumin, garlic powder, chili powder, oregano, parsley, paprika, and pepper.
3. Brush cod fillets with oil and rub with spice mixture and place in the refrigerator for 30 minutes.
4. Preheat the cosori air fryer to 380 F.
5. Bring cod fillets in the air fryer basket then cook for 8-13 minutes or until the

internal temperature of fish fillet reaches 145 F.
6. Garnish fish fillets with lime zest and serve.

Per serving: Calories: 161kcal; Fat: 8.4g; Carbs: 2.3g; Protein: 20.5g

78. Simple & Perfect Shrimp

Preparation time: 10 minutes
Cooking time: 8 minutes
Servings: 4
Ingredients:

- 1 lb large shrimp, peeled, deveined, and tails removed
- 2 tbsp parmesan cheese, grated
- 1/2 tsp garlic granules
- 1 tsp fresh lemon juice
- 1 tbsp butter, melted
- Pepper
- Salt

Directions:

1. Line air fryer basket with parchment paper.
2. In a mixing bowl, mix together garlic, lemon juice, butter, pepper, and salt. Add shrimp and toss to coat.
3. Add shrimp into the air fryer basket and top with parmesan cheese.
4. Cook shrimp at 400 F for 8 minutes.
5. Serve and enjoy.

Per serving: Calories: 140kcal; Fat: 4.4g; Carbs: 2.5g; Protein: 23.6g

79. Tasty Shrimp Fajitas

Preparation time: 10 minutes
Cooking time: 22 minutes
Servings: 12
Ingredients:

- 1 lb shrimp, tail-off
- 2 tbsp taco seasoning
- 1/2 cup onion, diced
- 1 green bell pepper, diced
- 1 red bell pepper, diced

Directions:

1. Spray air fryer basket with cooking spray.
2. Add shrimp, taco seasoning, onion, and bell peppers into the mixing bowl and toss well.
3. Place shrimp mixture into the air fryer basket then cook at 390 F for 12 minutes.
4. Stir shrimp mixture and cook for 10 minutes more.
5. Serve and enjoy.

Per serving: Calories: 55kcal; Fat: 0.8g; Carbs: 2.7g; Protein: 9g

80. Parmesan White Fish Fillets

Preparation time: 10 minutes
Cooking time: 10 minutes
Servings: 4
Ingredients:

- 1 lb white fish fillets
- 1/2 tsp lemon pepper seasoning
- 1/4 cup parmesan cheese
- 1/4 cup coconut flour

Directions:

1. In a shallow dish, mix together coconut flour, parmesan cheese, and lemon pepper seasoning.
2. Spray white fish fillets from both sides with cooking spray.
3. Coat fish fillets with coconut flour mixture.
4. Place coated fish fillets into the air fryer basket then cook at 400 F for 10 minutes. Turn fish fillets halfway through.
5. Serve and enjoy.

Per serving: Calories: 220kcal; Fat: 10g; Carbs: 0.9g; Protein: 29.9g

81. Delicious Fish Bites

Preparation time: 10 minutes
Cooking time: 10 minutes
Servings: 4
Ingredients:

- 10 oz haddock
- 1 tsp paprika
- 1 tsp onion powder
- 1 tbsp dill pickle relish
- 1 tbsp mayonnaise
- 1/4 cup coconut flour
- 2 eggs, lightly beaten
- Pepper
- Salt

Directions:

1. Add fish fillet into the food processor and process until a paste is formed.
2. Add remaining ingredients and process for 1 minute.
3. Place mixture into the refrigerator for 10 minutes.
4. Make small balls from mixture and place into the air fryer basket. Spray the top of fish balls.
5. Cook at 350 F for 10 minutes. Turn halfway through.
6. Serve and enjoy.

Per serving: Calories: 138kcal; Fat: 4.3g; Carbs: 3.7g; Protein: 20.3g

82. Healthy Salmon Patties

Preparation time: 10 minutes
Cooking time: 7 minutes
Servings: 2
Ingredients:

- 8 oz salmon fillet, minced
- 1/4 tsp garlic powder
- 1 egg, lightly beaten
- 1 lemon, sliced
- 1/8 tsp salt

Directions:

1. In a bowl, mix together mince salon, garlic powder, egg, and salt until well combined.
2. Make two patties from the salmon mixture.
3. Preheat the cosori air fryer to 390 F.
4. Place lemon sliced lemon on the bottom of the air fryer basket then place salmon patties on top.
5. Cook salmon patties for 7 minutes.
6. Serve and enjoy.

Per serving: Calories: 191kcal; Fat: 9.3g; Carbs: 3.1g; Protein: 25.2g

83. Old Bay Seasoned Crab Cakes

Preparation time: 10 minutes
Cooking time: 10 minutes
Servings: 5
Ingredients:

- 2 eggs
- 1/4 cup almond flour
- 2 tsp dried parsley
- 1 tbsp dried celery
- 1 tsp old bay seasoning
- 1 1/2 tbsp Dijon mustard
- 2 1/2 tbsp mayonnaise
- 18 oz can lump crab meat, drained
- 1/2 tsp salt

Directions:

1. Line air fryer basket with aluminum foil.
2. Add all ingredients into the mixing bowl and mix until well combined. Place mixture in the refrigerator for 10 minutes.
3. Make five equal shapes of patties from mixture and place onto the aluminum foil in the air fryer basket.
4. Cook at 320 F for 10 minutes. Turn patties halfway through.

5. Serve and enjoy.

Per serving: Calories: 139kcal; Fat: 13.3g; Carbs: 4.2g; Protein: 17.6g

84. Quick & Easy Salmon

Preparation time: 10 minutes
Cooking time: 12 minutes
Servings: 2
Ingredients:

- 2 salmon fillets
- 1/2 tsp hot sauce
- 3 tbsp coconut aminos
- 1 garlic clove, minced
- 1 tsp ginger, grated
- 1 tsp sesame seeds, toasted

Directions:

1. Add salmon fillets into the zip-lock bag.
2. Mix together hot sauce, coconut aminos, garlic, and ginger and pour over salmon. Seal bag and place in the refrigerator for 30 minutes.
3. Place marinated salmon fillets into the air fryer basket then cook at 400 F for 6 minutes.
4. Turn salmon and brush with marinade and cook for 6 minutes more or until cooked.
5. Serve and enjoy.

Per serving: Calories: 272kcal; Fat: 11.8g; Carbs: 6g; Protein: 35g

85. Asian Salmon Steak

Preparation time: 10 minutes
Cooking time: 18 minutes
Servings: 2
Ingredients:

- 2 salmon steaks
- 2 tbsp sesame oil
- 3 tbsp garlic paste
- 2 tbsp rice vinegar
- 3 tbsp Worcestershire sauce
- 1/2 tsp kosher salt

Directions:

1. Add salmon steaks into the zip-lock bag.
2. In a small bowl, mix together sesame oil, garlic paste, vinegar, Worcestershire sauce, and salt and pour over salmon steaks.
3. Seal ziplock bag and place in the refrigerator for 1 hour.
4. Spray air fryer basket with cooking spray.
5. Remove salmon steaks from marinade and place it into the air fryer basket.
6. Cook at 400 F for 15 minutes. Turn salmon steaks and brush with reserved marinade and cook for 3 minutes more.
7. Serve and enjoy.

Per serving: Calories: 343kcal; Fat: 21.7g; Carbs: 8.7g; Protein: 26g

CHAPTER 5: Meat

86. Tasty Ginger Garlic Beef

Preparation time: 10 minutes
Cooking time: 20 minutes
Servings: 4
Ingredients:

- 1 lb beef tips, sliced
- 1 tbsp ginger, sliced
- 2 tbsp garlic, minced
- 2 tbsp sesame oil
- 1 tbsp fish sauce
- 2 tbsp coconut aminos
- 1 tsp xanthan gum
- 1/4 cup scallion, chopped
- 2 red chili peppers, sliced
- 2 tbsp water

Directions:

1. Spray air fryer basket with cooking spray.
2. Toss beef with xanthan gum together.
3. Add beef into the air fryer basket then cook at 390F for 20 minutes. Turn halfway through.
4. Meanwhile, in a saucepan add remaining ingredients except for green onion and heat over low heat. Once it begins boiling then remove from heat.
5. Add cooked meat into the saucepan and stir to coat. Let sit in the saucepan for 5 minutes.
6. Transfer in serving dish and top with green onion and serve.

Per serving: Calories: 349kcal; Fat: 21.9g; Carbs: 5.7g; Protein: 31.4g

87. Easy Greek Lamb Chops

Preparation time: 10 minutes
Cooking time: 10 minutes
Servings: 4
Ingredients:

- 2 lbs lamb chops
- 2 tsp garlic, minced
- 2 tsp dried oregano
- 1/4 cup fresh lemon juice
- 1/4 cup olive oil
- Pepper
- Salt

Directions:

1. In a mixing bowl, mix together lemon juice, oil, oregano, garlic, pepper, and salt. Add lamb chops to the bowl and coat well.
2. Add lamb chops into the air fryer basket then cook at 400 F for 10 minutes. Turn halfway through.
3. Serve and enjoy.

Per serving: Calories: 538kcal; Fat: 29.4g; Carbs: 1.3g; Protein: 64g

88. Garlicky Beef & Broccoli

Preparation time: 10 minutes
Cooking time: 25 minutes
Servings: 2
Ingredients:

- 1/2 lb beef stew meat, cut into pieces
- 2 garlic cloves, minced
- 1 tbsp olive oil
- 1/2 cup broccoli florets
- 1 onion, sliced
- 1 tbsp vinegar
- Pepper
- Salt

Directions:
1. Add meat and remaining ingredients into the large bowl and toss well.
2. Add meat mixture into the air fryer basket then cook at 390 F for 25 minutes. Press start.
3. Serve and enjoy.

Per serving: Calories: 307kcal; Fat: 14.2g; Carbs: 7.7g; Protein: 35.9g

89. Creole Seasoned Pork Chops

Preparation time: 10 minutes
Cooking time: 12 minutes
Servings: 6
Ingredients:

- 1 1/2 lbs pork chops, boneless
- 1 tsp garlic powder
- 1/4 cup parmesan cheese, grated
- 1/3 cup almond flour
- 1 tsp paprika
- 1 tsp Creole seasoning

Directions:
1. Spray air fryer basket with cooking spray.
2. Preheat the cosori air fryer to 360 F.
3. Add all ingredients except pork chops into the zip-lock bag.
4. Add pork chops into the bag. Seal bag and shake well.
5. Remove pork chops from the zip-lock bag and place it into the air fryer basket then cook for 12 minutes.
6. Serve and enjoy.

Per serving: Calories: 388kcal; Fat: 29.9g; Carbs: 1g; Protein: 27.3g

90. Dash Seasoned Pork Chops

Preparation time: 10 minutes
Cooking time: 20 minutes
Servings: 2
Ingredients:

- 2 pork chops, boneless
- 1 tbsp dash seasoning
- Pepper
- Salt

Directions:
1. Spray air fryer basket with cooking spray.
2. Rub seasoning all over the pork chops.
3. Bring seasoned pork chops into the air fryer basket then cook at 360 F for 20 minutes. Turn halfway through.
4. Serve and enjoy.

Per serving: Calories: 256kcal; Fat: 19.9g; Carbs: 0g; Protein: 18g

91. Moist Lamb Roast

Preparation time: 10 minutes
Cooking time: 1 hour 30 minutes
Servings: 4
Ingredients:

- 2.75 lbs lamb leg roast, make slits on top of the meat
- 2 garlic cloves, sliced
- 1 tbsp olive oil
- 1 tbsp dried rosemary
- Pepper
- Salt

Directions:
1. Stuff sliced garlic into the slits. Season with pepper and salt.
2. Mix together oil and rosemary and rub all over the meat.
3. Place meat into the air fryer basket then cook at 400 F for 15 minutes.
4. Turn temperature to 320 F for 1 hour 15 minutes.
5. Serve and enjoy.

Per serving: Calories: 670kcal; Fat: 45g; Carbs: 1.1g; Protein: 58.1g

92. Quick & Easy Lamb Chops

Preparation time: 10 minutes

Cooking time: 5 minutes
Servings: 2
Ingredients:

- 4 lamb chops
- 1/2 tbsp fresh oregano, chopped
- 1 1/2 tbsp olive oil
- 1 garlic clove, minced
- Pepper
- Salt

Directions:

1. Preheat the cosori air fryer to 400 F.
2. Mix together garlic, olive oil, oregano, pepper, and salt and rub all over lamb chops.
3. Place lamb chops into the air fryer basket then cook for 5 minutes.
4. Serve and enjoy.

Per serving: Calories: 514kcal; Fat: 27.1g; Carbs: 1.3g; Protein: 63.4g

93. Delicious Zaatar Lamb Chops

Preparation time: 10 minutes
Cooking time: 10 minutes
Servings: 4
Ingredients:

- 8 lamb chops, trimmed
- 1 tbsp zaatar
- 1/2 lemon
- 1 tsp olive oil
- 2 garlic cloves, crushed
- Pepper
- Salt

Directions:

1. Preheat the cosori air fryer to 400 F.
2. Rub lamb chops with garlic and oil.
3. Squeeze lemon juice over lamb chops and season with zaatar, pepper, and salt.
4. Place lamb chops into the air fryer basket then cook for 10 minutes. Turn halfway through.
5. Serve and enjoy.

Per serving: Calories: 435kcal; Fat: 17.9g; Carbs: 1.2g; Protein: 63.4g

94. Cheese Garlicky Pork Chops

Preparation time: 10 minutes
Cooking time: 20 minutes
Servings: 8
Ingredients:

- 8 pork chops, boneless
- 3/4 cup parmesan cheese
- 2 tbsp butter, melted
- 2 tbsp coconut oil
- 1 tsp thyme
- 1 tbsp parsley
- 5 garlic cloves, minced
- 1/4 tsp pepper
- 1/2 tsp sea salt

Directions:

1. Spray air fryer basket with cooking spray.
2. Preheat the cosori air fryer to 400 F.
3. In a bowl, mix together butter, spices, parmesan cheese, and coconut oil.
4. Brush butter mixture on top of pork chops and place it into the air fryer basket then cook for 20 minutes. Turn pork chops halfway through.
5. Serve and enjoy.

Per serving: Calories: 344kcal; Fat: 28.2g; Carbs: 1.1g; Protein: 21.2g

95. Baked Lamb Chops

Preparation time: 10 minutes
Cooking time: 30 minutes
Servings: 4
Ingredients:

- 4 lamb chops

- 1 1/2 tsp tarragon
- 1 1/2 tsp ginger
- 1 tsp garlic powder
- 1 tsp ground cinnamon
- Pepper
- Salt

Directions:
1. Add garlic powder, cinnamon, tarragon, ginger, pepper, and salt into the zip-lock bag and mix well. Add lamb chops in a bag.
2. Seal bag shake well and place it in the fridge for 2 hours.
3. Place marinated lamb chops into the air fryer basket then cook at 375 F for 20 minutes.
4. Turn lamb chops and cook for 10 minutes more.
5. Serve and enjoy.

Per serving: Calories: 216kcal; Fat: 8.3g; Carbs: 1.6g; Protein: 31.8g

96. Cheese Butter Steak

Preparation time: 10 minutes
Cooking time: 8 minutes
Servings: 2
Ingredients:

- 2 ribeye steaks
- 2 tbsp blue cheese butter
- 1 tsp black pepper
- 2 tsp garlic powder
- 2 tsp kosher salt

Directions:
1. Preheat the cosori air fryer to 400 F.
2. Spray air fryer basket with cooking spray.
3. Mix together garlic powder, pepper, and salt and rub all over the steaks.
4. Place steak in the air fryer basket then cook for 8 minutes. Turn steak halfway through.
5. Top with blue butter cheese and serve.

Per serving: Calories: 222kcal; Fat: 15g; Carbs: 4.1g; Protein: 18g

97. Tasty Steak Fajitas

Preparation time: 10 minutes
Cooking time: 15 minutes
Servings: 6
Ingredients:

- 1 lb steak, sliced
- 1/2 cup onion, sliced
- 3 bell peppers, sliced
- 1 tbsp olive oil
- 1 tbsp fajita seasoning, gluten-free

Directions:
1. Line air fryer basket with aluminum foil.
2. Add all ingredients large bowl and toss until well coated.
3. Transfer fajita mixture into the air fryer basket then cook at 390 F for 5 minutes.
4. Toss and cook for 5-10 minutes more.
5. Serve and enjoy.

Per serving: Calories: 199kcal; Fat: 6.3g; Carbs: 6.4g; Protein: 28g

98. Crispy Pork Chops

Preparation time: 10 minutes
Cooking time: 20 minutes
Servings: 4
Ingredients:

- 4 pork chops, boneless
- 2 eggs, lightly beaten
- 1 cup almond flour
- 1/4 cup parmesan cheese, grated
- 1 tbsp onion powder
- 1 tbsp garlic powder
- 1/2 tbsp black pepper
- 1/2 tsp sea salt

Directions:

1. Spray air fryer basket with cooking spray.
2. Preheat the cosori air fryer to 350 F.
3. In a shallow bowl, mix together almond flour, parmesan cheese, onion powder, garlic powder, pepper, and salt.
4. Whisk eggs in a shallow dish.
5. Dip pork chops into the egg then coat with almond flour mixture.
6. Place coated pork chops into the air fryer basket then cook for 20 minutes. Turn pork chops halfway through.
7. Serve and enjoy.

Per serving: Calories: 363kcal; Fat: 27g; Carbs: 5.3g; Protein: 24.9g

99. Herb Cheese Pork Chops

Preparation time: 10 minutes
Cooking time: 9 minutes
Servings: 2
Ingredients:

- 2 pork chops, boneless
- 1 tsp paprika
- 3 tbsp parmesan cheese, grated
- 1/3 cup almond flour
- 1/2 tsp Cajun seasoning
- 1 tsp herb de Provence

Directions:

1. Preheat the cosori air fryer to 350 F.
2. Mix together almond flour, Cajun seasoning, herb de Provence, paprika, and parmesan cheese. Spray pork chops with cooking spray.
3. Coat pork chops with almond flour mixture and place into the air fryer basket then cook for 9 minutes.
4. Serve and enjoy.

Per serving: Calories: 360kcal; Fat: 27.3g; Carbs: 2.4g; Protein: 26.7g

100. Thyme Lamb Chops

Preparation time: 10 minutes
Cooking time: 12 minutes
Servings: 4
Ingredients:

- 4 lamb chops
- 3 tbsp olive oil
- 1 tbsp dried thyme
- 3 garlic cloves, minced
- Pepper
- Salt

Directions:

1. Preheat the cosori air fryer to 390 F.
2. In a small bowl, mix together thyme, oil, and garlic.
3. Season lamb chops with pepper and salt and rubs with thyme oil mixture.
4. Place chops into the air fryer basket then cook for 12 minutes. Turn halfway through.
5. Serve and enjoy.

Per serving: Calories: 305kcal; Fat: 18.8g; Carbs: 1.2g; Protein: 31.8g

101. Flavorful Beef Roast

Preparation time: 10 minutes
Cooking time: 45 minutes
Servings: 8
Ingredients:

- 2 1/2 lbs beef roast
- 1/2 tsp onion powder
- 1 tsp rosemary
- 1 tsp dill
- 2 tbsp olive oil
- 1/2 tsp black pepper
- 1/2 tsp garlic powder

Directions:

1. Preheat the cosori air fryer to 360 F.

2. Mix together black pepper, garlic powder, onion powder, rosemary, dill, and olive oil. Rub all over the beef roast.
3. Bring beef roast in the air fryer basket then cook for 45 minutes.
4. Serve and enjoy.

Per serving: Calories: 296kcal; Fat: 12.4g; Carbs: 0.5g; Protein: 43.1g

102. Garlic Lemon Pork Chops

Preparation time: 10 minutes
Cooking time: 20 minutes
Servings: 5
Ingredients:

- 2 lbs pork chops
- 2 tbsp fresh lemon juice
- 2 tbsp garlic, minced
- 1 tbsp fresh parsley
- 1 1/2 tbsp olive oil
- Pepper
- Salt

Directions:
1. In a small bowl, mix together garlic, parsley, olive oil, and lemon juice. Season pork chops with pepper and salt.
2. Pour garlic mixture over the pork chops and coat well and allow to marinate for 30 minutes.
3. Add marinated pork chops into the air fryer basket then cook at 400 F for 20 minutes. Turn pork chops halfway through.
4. Serve and enjoy.

Per serving: Calories: 623kcal; Fat: 49.4g; Carbs: 1.3g; Protein: 41.1g

103. Coconut Butter Pork Chops

Preparation time: 10 minutes
Cooking time: 15 minutes
Servings: 2
Ingredients:

- 4 pork chops
- 1 tbsp coconut oil
- 1 tbsp coconut butter
- 2 tsp parsley
- 2 tsp garlic, grated
- Pepper
- Salt

Directions:
1. Preheat the cosori air fryer to 350 F.
2. In a large bowl, mix together garlic, butter, coconut oil, parsley, pepper, and salt.
3. Rub garlic mixture over the pork chops. Wrap marinated pork chops into the foil and place it in the refrigerator for 1 hour.
4. Remove pork chops from foil and place into the air fryer basket then cook for 15 minutes. Turn pork chops after 7 minutes.
5. Serve and enjoy.

Per serving: Calories: 686kcal; Fat: 57.1g; Carbs: 5g; Protein: 37.2g

104. Flavors Burger Patties

Preparation time: 10 minutes
Cooking time: 10 minutes
Servings: 8
Ingredients:

- 1 lb ground beef
- 1/4 cup ketchup
- 1/4 cup coconut flour
- 1/2 cup almond flour
- 1 garlic clove, minced
- 1/4 cup onion, chopped
- 2 eggs, lightly beaten
- 1/2 tsp dried tarragon
- 1 tsp Italian seasoning
- 1 tbsp Worcestershire sauce
- 1/4 tsp pepper

- 1/2 tsp sea salt

Directions:
1. Spray air fryer basket with cooking spray
2. Add all ingredients into the mixing bowl and mix until well combined.
3. Make 8 equal shape of patties from mixture and place on a plate. Place in refrigerator for 10 minutes.
4. Preheat the cosori air fryer to 360 F.
5. Place prepared patties in the air fryer basket then cook for 10 minutes.
6. Serve and enjoy.

Per serving: Calories: 146kcal; Fat: 5.8g; Carbs: 3.6g; Protein: 19.2g

105. Tender Pork Chops

Preparation time: 10 minutes
Cooking time: 13 minutes
Servings: 4
Ingredients:

- 4 pork chops, boneless
- 1/2 tsp granulated garlic
- 1/2 tsp celery seeds
- 1/2 tsp parsley
- 1/2 tsp granulated onion
- 2 tsp olive oil
- 1/2 tsp salt

Directions:
1. Spray air fryer basket with cooking spray.
2. In a small bowl, mix together with seasonings and sprinkle over the pork chops.
3. Bring pork chops into the air fryer basket then cook at 350 F for 5 minutes. Turn pork chops and cook for 8 minutes more.
4. Serve and enjoy.

Per serving: Calories: 278kcal; Fat: 22.3g; Carbs: 0.4g; Protein: 18.1g

106. Lime Cumin Beef

Preparation time: 10 minutes
Cooking time: 25 minutes
Servings: 4
Ingredients:

- 1 lb beef stew meat, cut into strips
- 1 garlic clove, minced
- 1/2 lime juice
- 1 tbsp olive oil
- 1/2 tbsp chives, chopped
- 1/2 tbsp ground cumin
- 1 tbsp garlic powder
- Pepper
- Salt

Directions:
1. Add the meat into the mixing bowl. Add remaining ingredients over meat and mix well.
2. Transfer meat into the air fryer basket then cook at 380 F for 25 minutes. Turn meat half way through.
3. Serve and enjoy.

Per serving: Calories: 253kcal; Fat: 10.8g; Carbs: 2.6g; Protein: 35g

107. Dried Herb Lamb Chops

Preparation time: 10 minutes
Cooking time: 8 minutes
Servings: 4
Ingredients:

- 1 lb lamb chops
- 1 tsp oregano
- 1 tsp thyme
- 1 tsp rosemary
- 2 tbsp fresh lemon juice
- 2 tbsp olive oil
- 1 tsp coriander
- 1 tsp salt

Directions:

1. Add all ingredients except lamb chops into the zip-lock bag. Add lamb chops to the zip-lock bag.
2. Seal bag and shake well and place it in the fridge overnight.
3. Place marinated lamb chops into the air fryer basket then cook at 390 F for 8 minutes. Turn lamb chops halfway through.
4. Serve and enjoy.

Per serving: Calories: 276kcal; Fat: 15.5g; Carbs: 0.8g; Protein: 32g

108. Asian Pork Chops

Preparation time: 10 minutes
Cooking time: 12 minutes
Servings: 2
Ingredients:

- 2 pork chops
- 1 tsp black pepper
- 3 tbsp lemongrass, chopped
- 1 tbsp shallot, chopped
- 1 tbsp garlic, chopped
- 1 tsp liquid stevia
- 1 tbsp sesame oil
- 1 tbsp fish sauce
- 1 tsp soy sauce

Directions:

1. Add pork chops in a mixing bowl. Pour remaining ingredients over the pork chops and mix well. Place in refrigerator for 2 hours.
2. Preheat the cosori air fryer to 400 F.
3. Place marinated pork chops into the air fryer basket then cook for 12 minutes. Turn pork chops after 7 minutes.
4. Serve and enjoy.

Per serving: Calories: 340kcal; Fat: 26.8g; Carbs: 5.3g; Protein: 19.3g

109. Easy & Delicious Pork Chops

Preparation time: 10 minutes
Cooking time: 15 minutes
Servings: 4
Ingredients:

- 4 pork chops
- 2 tsp parsley
- 2 tsp garlic, grated
- 1/4 tsp garlic powder
- 1/4 tsp onion powder
- 1 tbsp olive oil
- 1 tbsp butter
- Pepper
- Salt

Directions:

1. Preheat the cosori air fryer to 350 F.
2. In a large bowl, mix together seasonings, garlic, butter, and oil.
3. Add pork chops to the bowl and mix well. Place in refrigerator overnight.
4. Place marinated pork chops into the air fryer basket then cook for 15 minutes. Turn pork chops after 7 minutes.
5. Serve and enjoy.

Per serving: Calories: 315kcal; Fat: 26.3g; Carbs: 0.8g; Protein: 18.2g

110. Steak with Mushrooms

Preparation time: 10 minutes
Cooking time: 18 minutes
Servings: 3
Ingredients:

- 1 lb steaks, cut into 1/2-inch cubes
- 2 tbsp butter, melted
- 8 oz mushrooms, sliced
- 1/2 tsp garlic powder
- 1 tsp Worcestershire sauce
- Pepper
- Salt

Directions:

1. Spray air fryer basket with cooking spray.

2. Add all ingredients into the large mixing bowl and toss well.
3. Preheat the cosori air fryer to 400 F.
4. Add steak mushroom mixture into the air fryer basket then cook for 15-18 minutes. Shake basket twice.
5. Serve and enjoy.

Per serving: Calories: 388kcal; Fat: 15.5g; Carbs: 3.2g; Protein: 57.1g

CHAPTER 6: Snacks and Appetizers

111. Crispy Zucchini Fries

Preparation time: 10 minutes
Cooking time: 10 minutes
Servings: 4
Ingredients:

- 2 medium zucchinis, cut into fries shapes
- 1/2 tsp garlic powder
- 1 tsp Italian seasoning
- 1/2 cup parmesan cheese, grated
- 1/2 cup almond flour
- 1 egg, lightly beaten
- Pepper
- Salt

Directions:

1. Spray air fryer basket with cooking spray.
2. In a shallow dish, mix together almond flour, cheese, Italians seasoning, garlic powder, pepper, and salt.
3. In a shallow bowl, add the egg.
4. Dip zucchini fries into the egg and coat with almond flour mixture.
5. Place coated zucchini fries into the air fryer basket then cook at 400 F for 10 minutes.
6. Serve and enjoy.

Per serving: Calories: 93kcal; Fat: 5.7g; Carbs: 4.8g; Protein: 7.4g

112. Cheese Stuffed Mushrooms

Preparation time: 10 minutes
Cooking time: 5 minutes
Servings: 3
Ingredients:

- 12 baby mushrooms
- 1 tsp chives, minced
- 4 oz cream cheese
- 2 tbsp butter, melted
- 4 bacon slices, cooked and crumbled
- Pepper
- Salt

Directions:

1. In a small bowl, mix together cream cheese, chives, butter, bacon, pepper, and salt.
2. Stuff cream cheese mixture into the mushrooms.
3. Place mushrooms into the air fryer basket then cook at 350 F for 5 minutes.
4. Serve and enjoy.

Per serving: Calories: 397kcal; Fat: 32.2g; Carbs: 10.6g; Protein: 21.1g

113. Ranch Zucchini Chips

Preparation time: 10 minutes
Cooking time: 15 minutes
Servings: 2
Ingredients:

- 1 egg
- 2 medium zucchinis, cut into thin slices
- 1 tsp ranch seasoning
- 1 tsp parsley
- 1 tsp dill
- Pepper
- Salt

Directions:

1. In a small bowl, mix together ranch seasoning, parsley, dill, pepper, and salt.
2. Brush zucchini slices with egg and sprinkle with ranch seasoning mix.
3. Arrange zucchini slices into the air fryer basket then cook at 380 F for 10 minutes.
4. Turn zucchini slices and cook for 5 minutes more.

5. Serve and enjoy.

Per serving: Calories: 69kcal; Fat: 2.6g; Carbs: 7.1g; Protein: 5.3g

114. Healthy Jicama Fries

Preparation time: 10 minutes
Cooking time: 20 minutes
Servings: 2
Ingredients:

- 2 cups jicama strips
- 1/2 tsp garlic powder
- 1/2 tsp paprika
- 2 tbsp olive oil
- 1/2 tsp onion powder
- 1/8 tsp cayenne
- 1/4 tsp chili powder

Directions:

1. Spray air fryer basket with cooking spray.
2. Add all ingredients into the mixing bowl and toss well to coat.
3. Add jicama strips into the air fryer basket then cook at 400 F for 20 minutes. Shake basket halfway through.
4. Serve and enjoy.

Per serving: Calories: 172kcal; Fat: 14.2g; Carbs: 12.5g; Protein: 1.3g

115. Easy Broccoli Nuggets

Preparation time: 10 minutes
Cooking time: 15 minutes
Servings: 4
Ingredients:

- 2 cups broccoli florets, cooked until soft
- 1 cup cheddar cheese, shredded
- 1/4 cup almond flour
- 2 egg whites
- 1/8 tsp salt

Directions:

1. Preheat the cosori air fryer to 325 F.
2. Spray air fryer basket with cooking spray.
3. Add cooked broccoli into the mixing bowl and mash using potato masher into the small pieces. Add remaining ingredients mix well to combine.
4. Make small nuggets from the broccoli mixture.
5. Place broccoli nuggets into the air fryer basket then cook for 15 minutes. Turn halfway through.
6. Serve and enjoy.

Per serving: Calories: 148kcal; Fat: 10.4g; Carbs: 3.9g; Protein: 10.5g

116. Easy Jalapeno Poppers

Preparation time: 10 minutes
Cooking time: 5 minutes
Servings: 5
Ingredients:

- 10 fresh jalapeno peppers, cut in half and remove seeds
- 1/4 cup cheddar cheese, shredded
- 6 oz cream cheese, softened
- 3 bacon slices, cooked and crumbled
- 1/4 tsp onion powder
- 1/4 tsp garlic powder

Directions:

1. Spray air fryer basket with cooking spray.
2. In a bowl, mix together bacon, cream cheese, garlic powder, onion powder, and cheddar cheese.
3. Stuff each jalapeno half with a bacon cheese mixture.
4. Place stuffed jalapeno peppers in the air fryer basket then cook at 370 F for 5 minutes.
5. Serve and enjoy.

Per serving: Calories: 216kcal; Fat: 18.9g; Carbs: 3.4g; Protein: 8.6g

117. Herb Roasted Carrots

Preparation time: 10 minutes
Cooking time: 20 minutes
Servings: 6
Ingredients:

- 2 lbs carrots, peeled and cut into fries shape
- 1 tsp dried thyme
- 3 tbsp olive oil
- 2 tbsp dried parsley
- 1 tsp dried oregano
- Pepper
- Salt

Directions:

1. Add carrots in a large bowl. Add remaining ingredients and toss well.
2. Add carrots fries into the air fryer basket then cook at 400 F for 20 minutes. Toss halfway through.
3. Serve and enjoy.

Per serving: Calories: 124kcal; Fat: 7.1g; Carbs: 15.2g; Protein: 1.3g

118. Healthy Zucchini Chips

Preparation time: 10 minutes
Cooking time: 30 minutes
Servings: 2
Ingredients:

- 2 medium zucchinis, cut into 1/4-inch thick slices
- 1/2 tsp garlic powder
- 1/2 cup parmesan cheese, grated
- 1 tbsp rosemary, chopped
- 1/4 cup olive oil
- Pepper
- Salt

Directions:

1. In a mixing bowl, toss zucchini slices with garlic powder, cheese, rosemary, oil, pepper, and salt.
2. Arrange zucchini slices into the air fryer basket then cook at 300 F for 30 minutes. turn halfway through.
3. Serve and enjoy.

Per serving: Calories: 255kcal; Fat: 31.2g; Carbs: 9.1g; Protein: 10.6g

119. Delicious Chicken Dip

Preparation time: 10 minutes
Cooking time: 20 minutes
Servings: 6
Ingredients:

- 2 cups chicken, cooked and shredded
- 7.5 oz cream cheese, softened
- 4 tbsp hot sauce
- 1/4 tsp garlic powder
- 3/4 cup sour cream
- 1/4 tsp onion powder

Directions:

1. Preheat the cosori air fryer to 325 F.
2. Add all ingredients in a mixing bowl and mix until well combined.
3. Pour mixture in air fryer safe dish.
4. Place dish in the air fryer basket then cook for 20 minutes.
5. Serve and enjoy.

Per serving: Calories: 258kcal; Fat: 19.8g; Carbs: 2.5g; Protein: 17.2g

120. Stuffed Jalapeno Poppers

Preparation time: 10 minutes
Cooking time: 7 minutes
Servings: 10
Ingredients:

- 10 jalapeno peppers, cut in half, remove seeds & membranes
- 1/4 tsp paprika
- 1/2 tsp chili powder
- 1 tsp ground cumin
- 1 tsp garlic powder
- 1/2 cup cheddar cheese, shredded

- 4 oz cream cheese
- 1 tsp salt

Directions:
1. In a small bowl, mix together cream cheese, cheddar cheese, garlic powder, cumin, chili powder, paprika, and salt.
2. Stuff cream cheese mixture into each jalapeno half.
3. Place stuffed jalapeno peppers into the air fryer basket then cook at 350 F for 7 minutes.
4. Serve and enjoy.

Per serving: Calories: 71kcal; Fat: 6.1g; Carbs: 1.8g; Protein: 2.6g

121. Simple Air Fried Vegetables

Preparation time: 10 minutes
Cooking time: 18 minutes
Servings: 4
Ingredients:

- 1 cup broccoli florets
- 1 cup carrots, sliced
- 1 cup cauliflower, cut into florets
- 1 tbsp olive oil
- Pepper
- Salt

Directions:
1. Add all vegetables in a large bowl. Drizzle with olive oil then season with pepper and salt.
2. Transfer vegetables to the air fryer basket then cook at 380 F for 18 minutes. Toss halfway through.
3. Serve and enjoy.

Per serving: Calories: 55kcal; Fat: 3.6g; Carbs: 5.6g; Protein: 1.4g

122. Flavorful Eggplant Slices

Preparation time: 5 minutes
Cooking time: 20 minutes
Servings: 4
Ingredients:

- 1 eggplant, cut into 1-inch slices
- 1/2 tsp red pepper
- 1 tsp garlic powder
- 1/2 tsp Italian seasoning
- 1 tsp paprika
- 2 tbsp olive oil
- 1/8 tsp cayenne

Directions:
1. Add all ingredients into the large bowl and toss well.
2. Place eggplant slices into the air fryer basket then cook at 375 F for 20 minutes. Turn eggplant slices halfway through.
3. Serve and enjoy.

Per serving: Calories: 99kcal; Fat: 7.5g; Carbs: 8.8g; Protein: 1.5g

123. Spicy Salmon Bites

Preparation time: 10 minutes
Cooking time: 12 minutes
Servings: 4
Ingredients:

- 1 lb salmon fillets, boneless and cubes
- 1/2 tsp chili powder
- 2 tsp olive oil
- 1/4 tsp cayenne pepper
- Pepper
- Salt

Directions:
1. Spray air fryer basket with cooking spray.
2. Add all ingredients into the bowl and toss well.

3. Arrange salmon cubes into the air fryer basket then cook at 350 F for 12 minutes. Turn halfway through.
4. Serve and enjoy.

Per serving: Calories: 171kcal; Fat: 9.4g; Carbs: 0.3g; Protein: 22.1g

124. Crab Stuffed Mushrooms

Preparation time: 10 minutes
Cooking time: 8 minutes
Servings: 16
Ingredients:

- 16 mushrooms, clean and chop stems
- 2 oz crab meat, chopped
- 8 oz cream cheese, softened
- 2 garlic cloves, minced
- 1/2 tsp chili powder
- 1/4 tsp onion powder
- 1/4 cup cheddar cheese, shredded
- 1/4 tsp pepper

Directions:

1. In a large bowl, mix together cheese, mushroom stems, chili powder, onion powder, pepper, crabmeat, cream cheese, and garlic until well combined.
2. Stuff mushrooms with cheese mixture.
3. Place stuffed mushrooms into the air fryer basket then cook at 370 F for 8 minutes.
4. Serve and enjoy.

Per serving: Calories: 65kcal; Fat: 5.7g; Carbs: 1.3g; Protein: 2.6g

125. Crispy Brussels sprouts

Preparation time: 10 minutes
Cooking time: 14 minutes
Servings: 2
Ingredients:

- 1/2 lb Brussels sprouts, trimmed and halved
- 1/2 tsp chili powder
- 1/4 tsp cayenne
- 1/2 tbsp olive oil
- Pepper
- Salt

Directions:

1. Add all ingredients into the large bowl and toss well.
2. Spread Brussels sprouts into the air fryer basket then cook at 370 F for 14 minutes. Toss halfway through.
3. Serve and enjoy.

Per serving: Calories: 82kcal; Fat: 4g; Carbs: 10.8g; Protein: 4g

126. Crispy Cauliflower Bites

Preparation time: 10 minutes
Cooking time: 15 minutes
Servings: 4
Ingredients:

- 1 lb cauliflower florets
- 1 tsp sesame seeds
- 1 tsp dried rosemary
- 1 1/2 tsp garlic powder
- 1 tbsp olive oil
- Pepper
- Salt

Directions:

1. Spray air fryer basket with cooking spray.
2. Add all ingredients into the bowl and toss well to coat.
3. Add cauliflower florets into the air fryer basket then cook at 400 F for 15 minutes. Shake basket halfway through.
4. Serve and enjoy.

Per serving: Calories: 67kcal; Fat: 4g; Carbs: 7.2g; Protein: 2.6g

127. Healthy Roasted Almonds

Preparation time: 5 minutes
Cooking time: 8 minutes
Servings: 8
Ingredients:

- 2 cups almonds
- 1 tbsp garlic powder
- 1 tbsp soy sauce
- 1/4 tsp pepper
- 1 tsp paprika
- Pinch of cayenne

Directions:

1. Spray air fryer basket with cooking spray.
2. Add pepper, paprika, garlic powder, cayenne, and soy sauce in a bowl and stir well. Add almonds and stir to coat.
3. Add almonds in the air fryer basket then cook at 320 F for 6-8 minutes. Shake basket after every 2 minutes.
4. Serve and enjoy.

Per serving: Calories: 143kcal; Fat: 11.9g; Carbs: 6.2g; Protein: 5.4g

128. Healthy Roasted Pecans

Preparation time: 10 minutes
Cooking time: 6 minutes
Servings: 6
Ingredients:

- 2 cups pecan halves
- 1 tbsp butter, melted
- Pepper
- Salt

Directions:

1. Preheat the cosori air fryer to 200 F.
2. Add pecans, butter, and salt in a bowl and toss well.
3. Transfer pecans into the air fryer basket then cook for 4-6 minutes. Toss after every 2 minutes.
4. Serve and enjoy.

Per serving: Calories: 307kcal; Fat: 31.7g; Carbs: 6g; Protein: 4.5g

129. Chicken Stuffed Poblanos

Preparation time: 10 minutes
Cooking time: 15 minutes
Servings: 6
Ingredients:

- 3 poblano peppers, cut in half & remove seeds
- 2 oz cheddar cheese, grated
- 1 1/2 cup spinach artichoke dip
- 1 cup chicken breast, cooked and chopped

Directions:

1. In a small bowl, mix together chicken, spinach artichoke dip, and half cheddar cheese.
2. Stuff chicken mixture into the poblano peppers.
3. Place stuffed poblano peppers into the air fryer basket. Sprinkle remaining cheese on top of peppers.
4. Cook at 350 F for 12-15 minutes.
5. Serve and enjoy.

Per serving: Calories: 91kcal; Fat: 5.6g; Carbs: 3g; Protein: 7.1g

130. Parmesan Carrot Fries

Preparation time: 10 minutes
Cooking time: 15 minutes
Servings: 4
Ingredients:

- 6 carrots, peeled and cut into fries shapes
- 2 tbsp parmesan cheese, grated
- 2 tbsp garlic, minced
- 2 tbsp olive oil
- Pepper
- Salt

Directions:
1. In a mixing bowl, toss carrot fries, parmesan cheese, garlic, oil, pepper, and salt.
2. Add carrot fries into the air fryer basket then cook at 350 F for 15 minutes. Turn fries halfway through.
3. Serve and enjoy.

Per serving: Calories: 126kcal; Fat: 8.5g; Carbs: 10.7g; Protein: 3.3g

CHAPTER 7: Desserts

131. Almond Butter Fudge Brownies

Preparation time: 10 minutes
Cooking time: 10 minutes
Servings: 4
Ingredients:

- 2 tbsp cocoa powder
- 1/4 tsp baking powder
- 1/2 tsp baking soda
- 2 tbsp unsweetened applesauce
- 15 drops liquid stevia
- 3 tbsp almond flour
- 1/2 tsp vanilla
- 1 tbsp unsweetened almond milk
- 1/2 cup almond butter
- 1 tbsp coconut oil, melted
- 1/4 tsp sea salt

Directions:

1. Preheat the cosori air fryer to 350 F.
2. Grease air fryer baking dish with cooking spray and set aside.
3. In a small bowl, mix together almond flour, baking powder, baking soda, cocoa powder, and salt. Set aside.
4. In a microwave-safe bowl, gently warm coconut oil and almond butter until melted.
5. Add stevia, vanilla, milk, and applesauce in the coconut oil mixture and stir well.
6. Add dry ingredients to the wet ingredients then stir to combine.
7. Pour batter into prepared dish.
8. Place dish into the air fryer basket then cook for 10 minutes.
9. Slice and serve.

Per serving: Calories: 173kcal; Fat: 15.4g; Carbs: 7.5g; Protein: 5.5g

132. Delicious Chocó Cookies

Preparation time: 10 minutes
Cooking time: 10 minutes
Servings: 20
Ingredients:

- 1 cup almond flour
- 1 cup almond butter
- 2 tbsp chocolate protein powder
- 3 tbsp ground chia

Directions:

1. Line air fryer basket with foil.
2. Preheat the cosori air fryer to 350 F.
3. In a huge bowl, add all ingredients and mix until well combined.
4. Make small balls from the mixture. Place some balls on foil in the air fryer basket. Press lightly down using the back of a fork.
5. Cook for 10 minutes. Cook remaining cookies in batches.
6. Allow to cool completely.
7. Serve and enjoy.

Per serving: Calories: 21kcal; Fat: 1.3g; Carbs: 0.7g; Protein: 1.9g

133. Yummy Brownie Muffins

Preparation time: 10 minutes
Cooking time: 15 minutes
Servings: 6
Ingredients:

- 3 eggs
- 1/3 cup unsweetened cocoa powder
- 1/2 cup Swerve
- 1 cup almond flour
- 1 tbsp gelatin
- 1/3 cup butter, melted

Directions:

1. Add all ingredients into the mixing bowl and stir until well combined.
2. Pour mixture into the mini silicone muffin molds.
3. Place molds into the air fryer basket then cook at 350 F for 10-15 minutes.
4. Serve and enjoy.

Per serving: Calories: 164kcal; Fat: 15.4g; Carbs: 4g; Protein: 5.8g

134. Blueberry Muffins

Preparation time: 10 minutes
Cooking time: 20 minutes
Servings: 12
Ingredients:

- 2 eggs
- 1/2 tsp vanilla
- 1/2 cups Swerve
- 16 oz cream cheese
- 1/4 cup almonds, sliced
- 1/4 cup blueberries

Directions:

1. Preheat the cosori air fryer to 350 F.
2. In a mixing bowl, beat cream cheese until smooth.
3. Add eggs, vanilla, and sweetener and beat until well combined.
4. Add almonds and blueberries and fold well.
5. Spoon mixture into the silicone muffin molds.
6. Place molds in the air fryer basket then cook for 20 minutes. Cook in batches.
7. Serve and enjoy.

Per serving: Calories: 156kcal; Fat: 14.9g; Carbs: 2g; Protein: 4.2g

135. Cinnamon Cappuccino Muffins

Preparation time: 10 minutes
Cooking time: 25 minutes
Servings: 12
Ingredients:

- 4 eggs
- 1 tsp espresso powder
- 1 tsp cinnamon
- 2 tsp baking powder
- 1/4 cup coconut flour
- 1/2 cup Swerve
- 2 cups almond flour
- 1/2 tsp vanilla
- 1/2 cup sour cream
- 1/4 tsp salt

Directions:

1. Preheat the cosori air fryer to 350 F.
2. Add sour cream, vanilla, espresso powder, and eggs in a blender and blend until smooth.
3. Add almond flour, cinnamon, baking powder, coconut flour, Swerve, and salt and blend to combine.
4. Pour mixture into the silicone muffin molds.
5. Place molds into the air fryer basket then cook for 25 minutes. Cook in batches.
6. Serve and enjoy.

Per serving: Calories: 151kcal; Fat: 12.9g; Carbs: 5.3g; Protein: 6.2g

136. Almond Cookies

Preparation time: 10 minutes
Cooking time: 12 minutes
Servings: 12
Ingredients:

- 1 cup almond flour
- 2 1/2 tbsp Swerve
- 1 tbsp water

- 2 tbsp coconut oil, melted
- Pinch of salt

Directions:
1. Preheat the cosori air fryer to 350 F.
2. Line air fryer basket with parchment paper.
3. Add all ingredients into the mixing bowl and mix until well combined.
4. Make 1-inch balls from mixture and place in an air fryer basket. In batches.
5. Using a fork flatten each ball and cook for 10-12 minutes.
6. Serve and enjoy.

Per serving: Calories: 34kcal; Fat: 3.4g; Carbs: 0.9g; Protein: 0.5g

137. Vanilla Almond Cinnamon Mug Cake

Preparation time: 5 minutes
Cooking time: 10 minutes
Servings: 1
Ingredients:

- 1 scoop vanilla protein powder
- 1/4 cup unsweetened almond milk
- 1/2 tsp baking powder
- 1/4 tsp vanilla
- 1 tsp Swerve
- 1/2 tsp cinnamon
- 1 tbsp almond flour

Directions:
1. Add protein powder, cinnamon, almond flour, sweetener, and baking powder into the mug and mix well.
2. Add vanilla and milk then stir well.
3. Place the mug in the air fryer basket then cook at 390 F for 10 minutes.
4. Serve and enjoy.

Per serving: Calories: 174kcal; Fat: 4.5g; Carbs: 6.7g; Protein: 28.8g

138. Lemon Cheese Muffins

Preparation time: 10 minutes
Cooking time: 14 minutes
Servings: 12
Ingredients:

- 3 eggs
- 1/4 cup coconut oil
- 1/4 cup ricotta cheese
- 1 cup almond flour
- 1 tsp lemon extract
- 1/4 cup heavy cream
- 4 true lemon packets
- 2 tbsp poppy seeds
- 1 tsp baking powder
- 1/3 cup Swerve

Directions:
1. Add all ingredients into the large mixing bowl and beat until fluffy.
2. Pour batter into the silicone muffin molds and place in the air fryer basket. In batches.
3. Cook at 320 F for 14 minutes or until cooked.
4. Serve and enjoy.

Per serving: Calories: 93kcal; Fat: 8.8g; Carbs: 1.6g; Protein: 2.8g

139. Choco Almond Butter Brownie

Preparation time: 10 minutes
Cooking time: 20 minutes
Servings: 4
Ingredients:

- 1 cup banana, overripe & mashed
- 1 scoop vanilla protein powder
- 1/2 tsp vanilla
- 2 tbsp unsweetened cocoa powder
- 1/2 cup almond butter, melted

Directions:
1. Preheat the cosori air fryer to 350 F.

2. Line baking dish with parchment paper and set aside.
3. Add all ingredients into the blender and blend until smooth.
4. Pour batter into the prepared dish.
5. Place dish into the air fryer basket then cook for 20 minutes.
6. Slice and serve.

Per serving: Calories: 81kcal; Fat: 1.6g; Carbs: 10.6g; Protein: 8.1g

140. Butter Cookies

Preparation time: 10 minutes
Cooking time: 10 minutes
Servings: 10
Ingredients:

- 3 tbsp butter, softened
- 1/4 cup Swerve
- 1/2 tsp vanilla
- 1 cup almond flour

Directions:

1. Preheat the cosori air fryer to 350 F.
2. Line air fryer basket with parchment paper.
3. Add all ingredients into the mixing bowl and mix until well combined.
4. Make 1-inch balls from mixture and place in an air fryer basket. In batches.
5. Using a fork flatten each ball and cook for 10 minutes.
6. Serve and enjoy.

Per serving: Calories: 47kcal; Fat: 4.9g; Carbs: 0.7g; Protein: 0.6g

141. Choco Mug Brownie

Preparation time: 5 minutes
Cooking time: 10 minutes
Servings: 1
Ingredients:

- 1 scoop chocolate protein powder
- 1/2 tsp baking powder
- 1/4 cup unsweetened almond milk
- 1 tbsp cocoa powder

Directions:

1. Add baking powder, protein powder, and cocoa powder in a heat-safe mug and mix well.
2. Add milk then stir well.
3. Bring the mug in the air fryer basket then cook at 390 F for 10 minutes.
4. Serve and enjoy.

Per serving: Calories: 79kcal; Fat: 2.4g; Carbs: 6.6g; Protein: 11.2g

142. Lemon Ricotta Cake

Preparation time: 10 minutes
Cooking time: 40 minutes
Servings: 8
Ingredients:

- 4 eggs
- 1 lemon juice
- 1 lb ricotta
- 1 lemon zest
- 1/4 cup Swerve

Directions:

1. Preheat the cosori air fryer to 325 F.
2. Spray air fryer baking dish with a cooking spray.
3. In a bowl, beat ricotta cheese until smooth. Whisk in the eggs one by one.
4. Whisk in lemon juice and zest. Pour batter into the prepared baking dish.
5. Place dish into the air fryer basket then cook for 40 minutes.
6. Slice and serve.

Per serving: Calories: 110kcal; Fat: 6.7g; Carbs: 3.1g; Protein: 9.2g

143. Delicious Chocolate Muffins

Preparation time: 10 minutes
Cooking time: 30 minutes
Servings: 10
Ingredients:

- 2 eggs, lightly beaten
- 1 tbsp baking powder, gluten-free
- 4 tbsp Swerve
- 1/2 cup unsweetened cocoa powder
- 1/2 cup cream
- 1/2 tsp vanilla
- 1 cup almond flour
- Pinch of salt

Directions:

1. Preheat the cosori air fryer to 375 F.
2. In a mixing bowl, mix together almond flour, baking powder, swerve, cocoa powder, and salt.
3. In a separate bowl, beat eggs with cream, and vanilla.
4. Pour egg mixture into the almond flour mixture and mix well.
5. Pour batter into the Silicone muffin molds.
6. Place molds into the air fryer basket then cook for 30 minutes. Cook in batches.
7. Serve and enjoy.

Per serving: Calories: 50kcal; Fat: 3.5g; Carbs: 4.9g; Protein: 2.7g

144. Chocolate Protein Brownie

Preparation time: 10 minutes
Cooking time: 15 minutes
Servings: 8
Ingredients:

- 1/2 tsp vanilla
- 3 tbsp coconut butter, melted
- 4 egg whites
- 2 scoops chocolate protein powder
- 3 tbsp unsweetened cocoa powder
- 1/4 cup Swerve
- 1/4 cup almond flour
- 1/4 tsp salt

Directions:

1. Preheat the cosori air fryer to 300 F.
2. Grease air fryer baking dish and set aside.
3. In a medium bowl, mix together all dry ingredients.
4. Add egg whites, vanilla, and melted coconut butter into the mixing bowl and beat until smooth.
5. Add dry mixture into the egg white mixture and mix until well combined.
6. Pour batter into the prepared dish.
7. Place dish into the air fryer basket then cook for 15 minutes.
8. Slice and serve.

Per serving: Calories: 70kcal; Fat: 4.5g; Carbs: 3.3g; Protein: 5.2g

145. Cream Cheese Brownies

Preparation time: 10 minutes
Cooking time: 20 minutes
Servings: 12
Ingredients:

- 6 eggs
- 2 tsp vanilla
- 1/2 tsp baking powder
- 2/3 cup unsweetened cocoa powder
- 1 1/2 sticks butter, melted
- 4 tbsp Swerve
- 4 oz cream cheese, softened

Directions:

1. Add all ingredients into the large bowl and beat until smooth using a hand mixer.
2. Pour mixture into the greased air fryer baking dish.

3. Place dish into the air fryer basket then cook at 350 F for 20 minutes.
4. Slice and serve.

Per serving: Calories: 181kcal; Fat: 17.6g; Carbs: 3.9g; Protein: 4.5g

146. Mozzarella Cheese Butter Cookies

Preparation time: 10 minutes
Cooking time: 12 minutes
Servings: 8
Ingredients:

- 2 eggs
- 1/3 cup mozzarella cheese, shredded
- 1 1/4 cup almond flour
- 5 tbsp butter, melted
- 1/3 cup sour cream
- 1/2 tsp baking powder
- 1/2 tsp salt

Directions:

1. Preheat the cosori air fryer to 370 F.
2. Add all ingredients into a huge bowl then mix using a hand mixer.
3. Spoon batter into the mini silicone muffin molds.
4. Place molds into the air fryer basket then cook for 12 minutes.
5. Serve and enjoy.

Per serving: Calories: 204kcal; Fat: 19.3g; Carbs: 4.4g; Protein: 5.8g

147. Moist Almond Muffins

Preparation time: 10 minutes
Cooking time: 15 minutes
Servings: 20
Ingredients:

- 1/2 cup coconut oil
- 1/2 cup almond flour
- 1/2 cup pumpkin puree
- 1/2 cup almond butter
- 1 tbsp cinnamon
- 1 tsp baking powder
- 2 scoops vanilla protein powder

Directions:

1. Preheat the cosori air fryer to 350 F.
2. In a huge bowl, mix together all dry ingredients.
3. Add wet ingredients into the dry ingredients and mix until well combined.
4. Pour batter into the silicone muffin molds and place in the air fryer basket. In batches.
5. Cook for 15 minutes.
6. Serve and enjoy.

Per serving: Calories: 68kcal; Fat: 6.1g; Carbs: 1.2g; Protein: 3g

148. Vanilla Custard

Preparation time: 10 minutes
Cooking time: 20 minutes
Servings: 2
Ingredients:

- 5 eggs
- 1/2 cup unsweetened almond milk
- 1/2 cup cream cheese
- 2 tbsp swerve
- 1 tsp vanilla

Directions:

1. Add eggs in a bowl and beat using a hand mixer.
2. Add cream cheese, sweetener, vanilla, and almond milk and beat for 2 minutes.
3. Spray two ramekins with cooking spray.
4. Pour batter into the prepared ramekins.
5. Preheat the cosori air fryer to 350 F.
6. Place ramekins into the air fryer basket then cook for 20 minutes.
7. Serve and enjoy.

Per serving: Calories: 381kcal; Fat: 32g; Carbs: 5.2g; Protein: 18.5g

149. Vanilla Mug Cake

Preparation time: 10 minutes
Cooking time: 10 minutes
Servings: 1
Ingredients:

- 1/4 cup unsweetened almond milk
- 1 scoop vanilla protein powder
- 1/2 tsp cinnamon
- 1/4 tsp vanilla
- 1 tsp Swerve
- 1 tbsp almond flour
- 1/2 tsp baking powder

Directions:

1. Add protein powder, Swerve, cinnamon, almond flour, and baking powder into the heat-safe mug and mix well.
2. Add vanilla and almond milk and stir well.
3. Place the mug in air fryer basket then cook at 390 F for 10 minutes
4. Serve and enjoy.

Per serving: Calories: 294kcal; Fat: 15g; Carbs: 11.2g; Protein: 33.3g

150. Cheesecake Muffins

Preparation time: 10 minutes
Cooking time: 20 minutes
Servings: 12
Ingredients:

- 2 eggs
- 16 oz cream cheese
- 1/2 tsp vanilla
- 1/2 cup Swerve
- 6 tbsp unsweetened cocoa powder

Directions:

1. Preheat the cosori air fryer to 350 F.
2. In a mixing bowl, beat cream cheese until smooth.
3. Add remaining ingredients and beat until well combined.
4. Spoon mixture into the silicone muffin molds.
5. Place molds in the air fryer basket then cook for 18-20 minutes. Cook in batches.
6. Serve and enjoy.

Per serving: Calories: 149kcal; Fat: 14.3g; Carbs: 2.6g; Protein: 4.3g

Conversion Chart

Volume Equivalents (Liquid)

US Standard	US Standard (ounces)	Metric (approximate)
2 tablespoons	1 fl. oz.	30 mL
¼ cup	2 fl. oz.	60 mL
½ cup	4 fl. oz.	120 mL
1 cup	8 fl. oz.	240 mL
1½ cups	12 fl. oz.	355 mL
2 cups or 1 pint	16 fl. oz.	475 mL
4 cups or 1 quart	32 fl. oz.	1 L
1 gallon	128 fl. oz.	4 L

Volume Equivalents (Dry)

US Standard	Metric (approximate)
⅛ teaspoon	0.5 mL
¼ teaspoon	1 mL
½ teaspoon	2 mL
¾ teaspoon	4 mL
1 teaspoon	5 mL
1 tablespoon	15 mL
¼ cup	59 mL
⅓ cup	79 mL
½ cup	118 mL
⅔ cup	156 mL
¾ cup	177 mL
1 cup	235 mL
2 cups or 1 pint	475 mL
3 cups	700 mL
4 cups or 1 quart	1 L

Oven Temperatures

Fahrenheit (F)	Celsius (C) (approximate)
250°F	120°C
300°F	150°C
325°F	165°C
350°F	180°C
375°F	190°C

400°F	200°C
425°F	220°C
450°F	230°C

Weight Equivalents

US Standard	Metric (approximate)
1 tablespoon	15 g
½ ounce	15 g
1 ounce	30 g
2 ounces	60 g
4 ounces	115 g
8 ounces	225 g
12 ounces	340 g
16 ounces or 1 pound	455 g

30-Day Meal Plan

Days	Breakfast	Lunch	Dinner	Dessert
1	Cheese Sausage Pepper Frittata	Dried Herb Lamb Chops	Asparagus With Almonds	Blueberry Muffins
2	Cheese Sausage Egg Muffins	Juicy & Tender Cod Fillets	Perfectly Spiced Chicken Tenders	Choco Almond Butter Brownie
3	Broccoli Bell Pepper Frittata	Curried Cauliflower With Pine Nuts	Garlic Lemon Pork Chops	Delicious Chocolate Muffins
4	Classic Sweet Potato Hash	Lemon Pepper Turkey Breast	Ginger Garlic Salmon	Delicious Chocó Cookies
5	Cheese Mushroom Egg Bake	Creole Seasoned Pork Chops	Parmesan Brussels Sprouts	Chocolate Protein Brownie
6	Delicious Chicken Burger Patties	Crisp Bacon Wrapped Scallops	Healthy Chicken & Broccoli	Almond Butter Fudge Brownies
7	Basil Feta Egg Bite	Air Fryer Basil Tomatoes	Herb Cheese Pork Chops	Mozzarella Cheese Butter Cookies
8	Easy Cheesy Breakfast Eggs	Flavorful Chicken Tenders	Healthy Salmon Patties	Choco Mug Brownie
9	Healthy Spinach Omelette	Moist Lamb Roast	Healthy Roasted Carrots	Vanilla Custard
10	Gruyere Cheese Egg Bite	Asian Salmon Steak	Crispy Crusted Chicken Tenders	Cinnamon Cappuccino Muffins
11	Breakfast Radish Hash Browns	Garlicky Cauliflower Florets	Cheese Garlicky Pork Chops	Vanilla Almond Cinnamon Mug Cake
12	Green Chilis Egg Bite	Flavors & Crisp Chicken Thighs	Tasty Shrimp Fajitas	Yummy Brownie Muffins
13	Cheddar Cheese Broccoli Egg Bite	Cheese Butter Steak	Asian Broccoli	Moist Almond Muffins
14	Bacon Cheese Egg Bites	Tasty Chipotle Shrimp	Quick & Easy Lemon Pepper Chicken	Cheesecake Muffins
15	Spinach Tomato Frittata	Easy & Crisp Brussels Sprouts	Tender Pork Chops	Cream Cheese Brownies
16	Breakfast Avocado Eggs	Creamy Pesto Chicken	Old Bay Shrimp	Lemon Ricotta Cake
17	Breakfast Cream Souffle	Steak With Mushrooms	Flavorful Tomatoes	Butter Cookies
18	Ham Egg Bites	Lime Garlic Shrimp Kababs	Flavors Dijon Chicken	Lemon Cheese Muffins

19	Cheese Ham Egg Cups	Balsamic Brussels Sprouts	Lime Cumin Beef	Almond Cookies
20	Cheese Omelet	Perfect Chicken Thighs Dinner	Perfectly Tender Frozen Fish Fillets	Vanilla Mug Cake
21	Mushroom Frittata	Coconut Butter Pork Chops	Easy Roasted Vegetables	Delicious Chocó Cookies
22	Cheesy Chicken Fritters	Parmesan White Fish Fillets	Turkey Spinach Patties	Choco Mug Brownie
23	Sausage Swiss Cheese Egg Bite	Healthy Squash & Zucchini	Flavorful Beef Roast	Vanilla Custard
24	Cheese Egg Frittata	Perfect Chicken Breasts	Old Bay Seasoned Crab Cakes	Cinnamon Cappuccino Muffins
25	Roasted Pepper Egg Bite	Crispy Pork Chops	Healthy Mixed Vegetables	Almond Butter Fudge Brownies
26	Breakfast Avocado Eggs	Quick & Easy Salmon	Nutritious Chicken & Veggies	Delicious Chocolate Muffins
27	Cheddar Cheese Broccoli Egg Bite	Crunchy Fried Cabbage	Delicious Zaatar Lamb Chops	Mozzarella Cheese Butter Cookies
28	Green Chilis Egg Bite	Chicken Spinach Meatballs	Simple & Perfect Shrimp	Vanilla Almond Cinnamon Mug Cake
29	Healthy Spinach Omelette	Easy Greek Lamb Chops	Easy Roasted Carrots	Chocolate Protein Brownie
30	Basil Feta Egg Bite	Flavorful Parmesan Shrimp	Juicy Lemon Pepper Chicken Thighs	Choco Almond Butter Brownie

Index

Air Fryer Basil Tomatoes; 22
Air Fryer Ratatouille; 24
Almond Butter Fudge Brownies; 58
Almond Cookies; 59
Asian Broccoli; 26
Asian Pork Chops; 49
Asian Salmon Steak; 41
Asparagus with Almonds; 22
Bacon Cheese Egg Bites; 14
Baked Lamb Chops; 44
Balsamic Brussels Sprouts; 21
Basil Feta Egg Bite; 19
Blueberry Muffins; 59
Breakfast Avocado Eggs; 19
Breakfast Cream Souffle; 16
Breakfast Radish Hash Browns; 15
Broccoli Bell Pepper Frittata; 13
Butter Cookies; 61
Cheddar Cheese Broccoli Egg Bite; 13
Cheese Butter Steak; 45
Cheese Egg Frittata; 19
Cheese Garlicky Pork Chops; 44
Cheese Ham Egg Cups; 15
Cheese Mushroom Egg Bake; 17
Cheese Omelet; 14
Cheese Sausage Egg Muffins; 12
Cheese Sausage Pepper Frittata; 14
Cheese Stuffed Mushrooms; 51
Cheesecake Muffins; 64
Cheesy Chicken Fritters; 18
Chicken Spinach Meatballs; 31
Chicken Stuffed Poblanos; 56
Chili Lime Cod; 38
Choco Almond Butter Brownie; 60
Choco Mug Brownie; 61
Chocolate Protein Brownie; 62
Cinnamon Cappuccino Muffins; 59
Classic Sweet Potato Hash; 16
Coconut Butter Pork Chops; 47
Crab Stuffed Mushrooms; 55
Cream Cheese Brownies; 62
Creamy Pesto Chicken; 32

Creole Seasoned Pork Chops; 43
Crisp Bacon Wrapped Scallops; 38
Crispy Brussels sprouts; 55
Crispy Cauliflower Bites; 55
Crispy Crusted Chicken Tenders; 33
Crispy Pork Chops; 45
Crispy Zucchini Fries; 51
Crunchy Fried Cabbage; 26
Curried Cauliflower with Pine Nuts; 23
Curried Eggplant Slices; 21
Dash Seasoned Pork Chops; 43
Delicious Chicken Burger Patties; 18
Delicious Chicken Dip; 53
Delicious Chocó Cookies; 58
Delicious Chocolate Muffins; 62
Delicious Fish Bites; 40
Delicious Zaatar Lamb Chops; 44
Dried Herb Lamb Chops; 48
Easy & Crisp Brussels Sprouts; 21
Easy & Delicious Pork Chops; 49
Easy Broccoli Nuggets; 52
Easy Cheesy Breakfast Eggs; 17
Easy Greek Lamb Chops; 42
Easy Jalapeno Poppers; 52
Easy Roasted Carrots; 23
Easy Roasted Vegetables; 23
Flavorful Beef Roast; 46
Flavorful Chicken Tenders; 31
Flavorful Eggplant Slices; 54
Flavorful Parmesan Shrimp; 37
Flavorful Tomatoes; 25
Flavors & Crisp Chicken Thighs; 32
Flavors Burger Patties; 47
Flavors Dijon Chicken; 27
Garlic Green Beans; 26
Garlic Lemon Pork Chops; 47
Garlic Yogurt Salmon Fillets; 35
Garlicky Beef & Broccoli; 42
Garlicky Cauliflower Florets; 22
Ginger Garlic Salmon; 37
Greek Meatballs; 33
Green Chilis Egg Bite; 12

Gruyere Cheese Egg Bite; 13
Ham Egg Bites; 18
Healthy Chicken & Broccoli; 30
Healthy Crab Cakes; 36
Healthy Jicama Fries; 52
Healthy Mixed Vegetables; 25
Healthy Roasted Almonds; 56
Healthy Roasted Carrots; 25
Healthy Roasted Pecans; 56
Healthy Salmon Patties; 40
Healthy Spinach Omelette; 15
Healthy Squash & Zucchini; 25
Healthy Zucchini Chips; 53
Herb Cheese Pork Chops; 46
Herb Roasted Carrots; 53
Juicy & Tender Cod Fillets; 36
Juicy Chicken Breasts; 29
Juicy Lemon Pepper Chicken Thighs; 32
Lemon Cheese Muffins; 60
Lemon Garlic White Fish; 35
Lemon Pepper Turkey Breast; 29
Lemon Ricotta Cake; 61
Lime Cumin Beef; 48
Lime Garlic Shrimp Kababs; 36
Moist Almond Muffins; 63
Moist Lamb Roast; 43
Mozzarella Cheese Butter Cookies; 63
Mushroom Frittata; 16
Nutritious Chicken & Veggies; 27
Old Bay Seasoned Crab Cakes; 40
Old Bay Shrimp; 35
Parmesan Brussels sprouts; 24
Parmesan Carrot Fries; 56

Parmesan White Fish Fillets; 39
Perfect Chicken Breasts; 28
Perfect Chicken Thighs Dinner; 27
Perfectly Spiced Chicken Tenders; 28
Perfectly Tender Frozen Fish Fillets; 37
Quick & Easy Lamb Chops; 43
Quick & Easy Lemon Pepper Chicken; 33
Quick & Easy Salmon; 41
Ranch Zucchini Chips; 51
Roasted Pepper Egg Bite; 12
Sausage Swiss Cheese Egg Bite; 19
Simple & Perfect Shrimp; 39
Simple Air Fried Vegetables; 54
Simple Vegan Broccoli; 21
Spiced Green Beans; 24
Spicy Salmon Bites; 54
Spinach Tomato Frittata; 17
Steak with Mushrooms; 49
Stuffed Jalapeno Poppers; 53
Tasty Chipotle Shrimp; 37
Tasty Ginger Garlic Beef; 42
Tasty Shrimp Fajitas; 39
Tasty Steak Fajitas; 45
Tasty Turkey Fajitas; 29
Tender & Juicy Cornish Hens; 33
Tender Pork Chops; 48
Tender Turkey Legs; 30
Thyme Lamb Chops; 46
Turkey Spinach Patties; 28
Vanilla Almond Cinnamon Mug Cake; 60
Vanilla Custard; 63
Vanilla Mug Cake; 64
Yummy Brownie Muffins; 58

Conclusion

The Cosori air fryer is an extremely popular kitchen appliance. It is the best method for preparing delicious and nutritious meals. It's exactly what you need when you want to prepare something delicious and savory for your loved ones but lack the time, skills, or energy to spend hours in the kitchen.

The Cosori air fryer will revolutionize your cooking techniques and become your new best friend in the kitchen.

If you already possess such a useful appliance, then this wonderful collection of recipes is all you need. The recipes collected in this incredible journal will surely impress you. They are all quick and simple to prepare with the Cosori air fryer, requiring only simple, readily available ingredients.

So, get to work immediately! Utilize the Cosori air fryer to prepare gourmet meals in the comfort of your own home.

Printed in Great Britain
by Amazon

Matthew Clark

SERIAL KILLERS

CANNIBALS

A Disturbing Journey in the Most Shocking True Crime Stories of Cannibalism

Copyright © 2021 publishing.

All rights reserved.

Author: Matthew Clark

No part of this publication may be reproduced, distributed or transmitted in any form or by any means, including photocopying recording or other electronic or mechanical methods or by any information storage and retrieval system without the prior written permission of the publisher, except in the case of brief quotation embodies in critical reviews and certain other non-commercial uses permitted by copyright law.

Table of Contents

Introduction 4

1. Peter Stumpp (Werewolf of Bedburg) 7

2. Zhang Yongming (The Cannibal Monster) 17

3. Philip Onyancha: The Vampire of Kenya 25

4. Albert Hamilton Fish: The Wolf of Wisteria 37

5. Joachim Kroll (The Ruhr Hunter) 51

6. Robin Gecht (Chicago Rippers Crew Leader) 63

7. Karl Denke 75

8. Albert Fentress (New York's Own Hannibal Lecter) 80

9. Jose Luis Calva Zepeda (The Cannibal Poet) 89

10. Alexander Spesivtsev 97

11. Alfred G. Packer (The Colorado Cannibal) 103

12. Andrei Chikatilo (The Red Ripper) 115

13. Boone Helm (The Kentucky Cannibal) 133

Conclusion 142

Introduction

Cannibalism is the act of one species consuming all or part of another. The term cannibalism derives from the Spanish word cannibal, meaning "a savage person who eats human flesh." Historically, indigenous people practiced cannibalism in response to starvation, especially after being driven from their land by colonialists.

In recent times, an increase in climate-related disasters has prompted widespread outbreaks of cannibalism around the world. Indigenous peoples such as the Inuit and Yanomamö (Abipones) have practiced cannibalism for centuries. However, it is unclear whether they did so before or after the Spanish invasion of South America. In "The Origins of Cannibalism," anthropologist Michael J. Harner argues that cannibalism was practiced in the New World, especially in areas with scarce food supply. He argued that this is due to their often belief that they were descended from cannibals.

However, there are cannibalism serial killers and victims in the U.S.A, UK and throughout the world- See Jeffrey Dahmer (murderer and cannibal), David Parker Ray (murderer and cannibals), John Wayne Gacy Jr. (mass murderer and cannibal). The flesh of the vanquished foe has been considered a great delicacy by many different cultures. Human flesh is generally perceived as having a flavor similar to pork. However, the flesh of an enemy such as one's rival or enemy has also been seen as taboo to eat, and the practice has been viewed as cannibalism.

Cannibalism is one of the crimes that fill people with the most hatred and disgust, with the mere thought of someone eating another human being causes many people to feel ill. Cannibalism is described as the basest of all crimes, and while some people may disagree, the act of cannibalism is an abomination of God. But some have become infamous due to their

However, there are recorded cases of cannibalism having been committed in our recent history. In this book, we will be looking at a list of the most notable cases of cannibalism relative to serial killers throughout the world. Now, let's get at it.

1. Peter Stumpp (Werewolf of Bedburg)

Peter Stumpp was a serial killer and a cannibal, dubbed the 'Werewolf of Bedburg,' during the 16th century. His murders were performed in a gruesome and inhuman way. He ravaged the body parts, ripped out the internal organs, chopped off the arms and legs, and in some cases, ate the unborn child inside a woman's body. His "favorites" were children, infants, women, and even livestock.

Peter Stumpp was a farmer in the small community of Bedburg, in Cologne, Germany, a city that was still a part of the Holy Roman Empire at that time. There is some confusion about Stumpp's real name, with the variations of Stubb or Stumpf, since it is believed to be coined because his left hand was severed. Some references state that his real name was Griswold. Stumpp was a respected figure of the community, apparently because of his incredible wealth and influence. His date of birth was unknown, but it is hypothesized that by the 1580s, his wife had already died, and he had two children, one girl and one boy.

Stumpp and his family lived in a time when there were conflicts between the Catholics and Protestants. The armies of both parties would meet in the heart of Bedburg, and encounters would usually leave casualties. Also, it was during that era when the Black Plague caused a large epidemic. Conflict and death were not uncommon in the region where Stumpp lived. Stumpp was a wealthy and decent man who lived with both his children and relatives to his fellow villagers. However, the truth was, he had an intimate relationship with one of his kin, and he constantly abused his daughter. The father-daughter incestuous relationship eventually resulted in the birth of a baby boy.

Despite the frequency of death and devastation in the area, one specific case arose the worry of the already anxious citizens. There were several deaths of livestock, especially cattle, and eventually, deaths of humans. At first, they thought that an enormous wolf caused them. The guts were usually ripped out, and the other body parts were chopped up and even spread around in different places. For 25 years, Stumpp wore a wolf's skin above his head. Those who have seen a glimpse of him described him as a wolf-like creature with huge eyes, a wide mouth, sharp teeth, massive paws, and a large and strong body frame. The killings continued for years, and at some point, people would travel through towns in groups of wagons laden with weapons. Sometimes, they would find severed body parts of the "werewolves" victims in fields and forests. Stumpp's attacks were varied, and he seemed not to care if his prey was an animal or a human. His victims were:

Livestock; Stumpp seemed to have taken a liking to cattle and cows. The farmers feared for the life of their livestock because they would often randomly find their cattle died in the fields. The cattle would lay on the ground, mutilated and viciously ripped open by some large and savage creature. Like lambs and calves, smaller animals were usually ripped open and devoured raw since their organs were often missing. The attacks lasted for years and years. At first, they suspected the attacks were from a large pack of wolves, but they never thought that a human, Peter Stumpp, could do the deeds. His attacks on the livestock were believed to have fueled Stumpp's desire to murder people, too.

Men and Women; Stumpp murdered both men and women but more of the latter. For young women, he first raped and abused them before he took their lives. Stumpp would then tear them apart. One case involved the killing of two men and a woman who were strolling outside the city. Stumpp was crouched behind the dark bushes, which completely hid him. He then pretended to call for help. The young man came to his aid, and when he did, Stumpp forcefully smashed his head with a large rock. Curious why his friend still hadn't returned, the other man went behind the bushes where he too was killed. The woman, who was shaking with fear, tried to run away but to no avail. She was also killed, but her body was never found, unlike the other two. Some hypothesize that Stumpp might have raped then killed the woman. On why her body was never recovered, it is assumed that Stumpp ate her completely.

Pregnant Women; In the course of Stumpp's slaughters, he murdered two pregnant women. After killing the women, Stumpp slashed their stomachs open and ripped the fetuses out of their mother's body with his bare hands. He would then proceed to eat the still-beating heart of the infant. According to Stumpp himself, he liked the taste of the hot and raw hearts of the infants, and he described them as exquisite snacks.

Children; When children disappeared from the farms and homes, their families would often assume that there was no chance that they would see their offspring alive. Dead children with excessively mutilated body parts were not an uncommon sight. Some of the children were never even found. According to the villagers, the children were strangled to death, beaten, and their throats were ripped open using bare hands or claws. Some of their bodies had the stomach ripped open, and their intestines and internal organs were partially eaten. In one case, one child was fortunate enough to survive the attack of the "werewolf." She played with her friends in the meadows among some cows and their calves when a large creature or man came after them. Stumpp eventually got hold of her, and he tried to gash the child's throat with his hands. Luckily, the child was wearing a high collar, and she had the chance to cry for help. The cows heard the girl's cries, and it startled them. The cattle then went after Stumpp. Another notable case of Stumpp's slaughter was that of his own family. The result of the incestuous relationship of Stumpp and his daughter Belle was a baby boy. Upon interrogation, Stumpp admitted that he killed his son. He detailed that he led his young son deep into the forest, beat him to death, and ate raw brains.

The villagers were certain that a ravaging animal, most probably a wolf, was on the loose. It caused numerous livestock deaths and deaths of women, children, and infants. Hunters set out to capture the animal, so they coursed the forests with dogs to pursue the culprit. According to one hunter, they chased and cornered a large wolf, but it changed into Peter Stumpp in front of their eyes. This side of the story is disputed, and the supposed "transformation" was just Peter Stumpp taking off his wolf hide. The hunters could not believe their eyes because Stumpp was a respectable man in the community. Nevertheless, he was brought to trial.

On October 28, 1589, Stumpp was found guilty of all the murders that he confessed to. His daughter and his mistress were also found guilty of being accomplices to the crimes. The three of them were sentenced to death, three days after, on All Hallows Eve of 1589. On October 31, 1589, the execution of Stumpp was noted as one of the most brutal executions in history. His body was laid and strapped on a wheel in a spread-eagled position. Metal pincers were heated until they were red hot, and flesh from ten different parts of his body was slowly pulled off his bones. His arms and legs were hit with the blunt end of an ax to break them completely and prevent him from crawling out of his grave. All of this was done while he was still alive. To finally kill him, he was beheaded, and his body was burnt in a big bonfire in the town square. His daughter and his mistress were also publicly executed and burnt on stakes beside Stumpp's body. The magistrate ordered a warning to potential devil worshipers to be erected on the site of Stumpp's execution. The wheel used to kill Stumpp was set on a high pole; 16 strips of wood were hung to represent all his victims, the wolf's body was placed on the very top, and above it, Stumpp's severed was put in place of the animal's head.

Hundreds of years after Peter Stumpp's killing spree, psychologists hypothesize that he was suffering from clinical lycanthropy, a kind of schizophrenic condition wherein a person experiences random bouts of neurosis, delusions, slurred and incoherent speech, and inappropriate and disordered behavior. Peter Stumpp's behavior can be explained as lycanthropic attacks wherein he lost his reason and eventually lost his mind. People who experience lycanthropy are people whose fears exceeded their coping mechanisms, making them project their fears onto other people.

2.Zhang Yongming (The Cannibal Monster)

China has a long history of cannibalism. In the 4th century, for example, it was quite common for harem girls to be slaughtered and served up as a delicacy to guests. During the 7th and 8th centuries Tang Dynasty, enemy soldiers were routinely used as a food source for an army on the march. In the 13th century, Marco Polo returned to Italy from his Far East expeditions with horror stories about human flesh consumption. And as recently as the 1800s, there were restaurants in China that served nothing but human flesh. More recently, the Communist state's disastrous "Great Leap Forward" of the late '50s and early 60's drove millions of ordinary citizens to cannibalism to survive.

China has also produced its fair share of cannibalistic killers, most notably Zhang Yongming, the so-called "Cannibal Monster." Over four years, from 2008 to 2012, Yongming strangled and dismembered at least 12 youths in the tiny village of Nanmen, later selling their dried flesh as "ostrich meat" in the local market.

Little is known about Zhang's early life. We first learn of his existence in 1979, when he was arrested for killing a man and mutilating his corpse. A conviction, in that case, saw him sentenced to death, but the punishment was subsequently reduced to life imprisonment. Paroled in September 1997, after serving just 16 years, Yongming was relocated to Nanmen, in southwest China's Yunnan province. There, he was given a tract of land and a meager government stipend and promptly forgotten about.

Zhang mainly kept to himself and hardly exchanged a word with anyone in the village. For their part, the villagers appear to have regarded him as a local eccentric who was best avoided. That is until young men, and teenage boys started going missing from the village.

At first, the distraught parents thought that their sons had been kidnapped to work as slave labor in the brick quarries. However, their appeals to local authorities brought a tepid response, and self-funded inquiries fared no better. Despite several parents spending their entire life savings on finding their sons, not a single one of the missing boys was found. They seemed simply to have vanished.

There were rumors, of course, clues even. Like the mysterious green garbage bags seen hanging outside Yongming's shack. Someone said they'd seen bones protruding from the bags, but no one seriously suspected the dim-witted farmer or the suspicious-looking dried meat he sold at the market.

Had any of the villagers known about Yongming's murderous past, they might have taken it more seriously when he looped a leather belt around a youth's neck in December 2011. Villagers who heard 17-year-old Zhang Jianyuan's screams and came rushing to his aid found Yongming with a leather belt drawn tightly around the boy's throat. The police were called, but Yongming laughed off the incident, insisting that he was only playing a prank on the boy. They believed him. Remarkably, given the spate of disappearances of young men from the area and Yongming's previous conviction for a mutilation murder, the police did not bother searching his house.

But even in a repressive country like China, the disappearances of over a dozen boys and young men from an area that spanned only two square miles could not be kept under wraps forever. Word eventually leaked to the media, and stories began to appear in the local press. These articles did not suggest that a serial killer was at large, but they put pressure on the Ministry of Public Security to take action. As a result, a team of investigators was sent to Nanmen. They almost immediately picked up a pattern to the disappearances. All of the victims had gone missing along a particular stretch of road, a path that led directly past Yongming's house.

The investigators began checking locations and talking to homeowners along the route. In those inquiries, they began to hear stories about the mysterious garbage bags hanging outside Yongming's home. According to at least one local, the bones they contained were human.

The investigative team laughed off those reports as superstitious nonsense, but they decided to visit him as Yongming's home was along the route anyway. They were in for a shock. The bags were hanging from Yongming's porch as described. They did contain bones, and those bones were unquestionably human.

After taking Yongming into custody, the officers searched his humble wooden shack. They were unprepared for what they found. Grisly chunks of human flesh hung from hooks, where they'd been left to dry. On a counter sat three large jars, each containing human eyeballs, floating in a semi-opaque fluid. More bones were scattered around the house and more still buried in a vegetable garden, which also held the decaying flesh of several of Yongming's victims. Under interrogation, Yongming admitted that he subsisted almost exclusively on human flesh and fed it to his dogs. What he couldn't eat, he salted and dried, selling it at the local market as "ostrich jerky."

Despite its lurid nature, Yongming's story was not the media sensation it might have been. The Chinese government denies the existence of serial killers within its borders and regulates the reporting of such cases. However, another aspect of the case did cause a media storm, the story of the local police's utterly incompetent handling of the case. Twenty people had gone missing from a tiny hamlet within the space of just two years. Yet with citizens up in arms, with local chatter rife about Yongming's activities, with Yongming's previous murder rap and arrest for trying to strangle a young man, the police did nothing. A judicial inquiry was launched into the case, resulting in 12 local officials, including the police chief, losing their jobs.

Zhang Yongming, meanwhile, went on trial and was unsurprisingly found guilty of murder and sentenced to death. This time there would be no reprieve for the depraved cannibal. On January 10, 2013, reports stated that Yongming had been escorted to a place of execution and executed.

3. Philip Onyancha: The Vampire of Kenya

Overview When Philip Onyancha, a Kenyan national, was in high school, he joined a cult whose aim was to murder a certain number of people. Onyancha was tasked with killing a hundred, but he only managed to kill 19 victims, primarily children and women. He claimed that the blame should not be on him but on the evil spirits that gave him the intense urge to kill. Onyancha, however, admitted having enjoyed drinking his victims' blood.

Early Life Philip Onyancha was born in 1978 in Kenya and was the son of a farmer, Samuel Onyancha, and Esther Onyancha. Onyancha went to school at the Kenyatta High School, where he was initially highly commended. According to his teachers, Onyancha used to be a brilliant boy at school. During his first year in high school, he topped his exams and was deemed an above-average student, always getting straight A's. His professors recalled that Onyancha talked eloquently and authoritatively, which made his classmates look up to him. He led the class in terms of academic achievements and, at the same time, extracurricular ones. Onyancha often represented his school in sports-related activities, such as ball games and athletics. His first year in high school turned out very promising, but when he reached the next level, there was something off about Onyancha's behavior. His mentors noted the decrease in the boy's competency, and they were surprised that he emerged with a C-minus in a very important examination. They recalled that everything went downhill after Onyancha was suspended for weeks because of a minor bullying incident. He was abruptly readmitted because of the lack of evidence, but he wasn't the same bright boy when he came back to school.

Cult and Kidnap Gang In reality, however, Onyancha confessed that his teacher encouraged him to join a cult in 1996. According to him, the cult would help him graduate faster and make him one of the wealthiest men in Kenya. Conversely, the cult system was for a member to kill 100 people so they could advance to the next level and meet the leader. His involvement with the dark organization was never known until he confessed to the police. Onyancha described the cult as an organization governed by evil spirits that gave them a special power to seduce, charm, or hypnotize people. His modus operandi was always to greet his victim first; the greeting serves as the start of the ritual, and the victim follows him wherever he wants. In a later admission, Onyancha confessed that he was under the influence of evil spirits in the act of killing. However, he did not know or see any other member of the said organization. Apart from being a part of a cult, Onyancha also claimed to be a gang member that kidnapped people and demanded a ransom from their families.

In some cases, their group would kill the victim but still demand a payout. His secret life as a kidnapper and a cult member went unnoticed since he was employed as a security guard who moved from station to station. His previous employer even commented that

Onyancha did not display any suspicious behavior during his service for the company. However, the truth was Onyancha was killed every time he was designated to a new service station.

Murders Overall, Onchanya admitted to killing 19 people in Thika, Karen, and nearby towns. According to him, his victims were usually women, the 'weaker sex,' and children - both powerless under his 'supernatural abilities.'Onyancha lured his victims to a secluded place, murdered them, mutilated them, and sometimes bit their necks and sucked their blood dry.

- **Random Women**

Catherine Chelengat

Catherine Chelengat was a worker in a water company in the suburb of Karen, Kenya. She was last seen near her relative's house early in November 2008. According to her relatives, she went out around 9 PM, which was the last they saw of her. Her family went looking for her for months, but the police had no leads on her whereabouts. Three months later, a man called her family demanding 30,000 Kenyan Shillings in exchange for Chelengat's safety. Her family begged the kidnapper for more time since they did not have that larger sum of money at that time. When they paid half of the ransom money, they were never contacted by the kidnappers again. Two years after Chelengat went missing, Onyancha led the police to the crime scene where he had performed the gruesome murder. According to him, in November 2008, he lured a woman unknown to him to one of the department stores in Karen.

Onyancha, then a security guard in the water company where Chelengat was an employee, greeted the woman and told her to follow him. They went inside the department store, and he led her to the stairs up to the roof. He said that the woman did not appear suspicious and blindly followed him. In the small ceiling compartment, Onyancha strangled Chelengat to death with his bare hands. He then bit her neck and sucked her blood. As Onyancha led the police to where he stashed the body, the police found a woman's body in an advanced stage of decomposition. The employees in the establishment were astonished that they never noticed a decaying body just above their heads. Onyancha told the police that he was confident that the body would not be found.

He murdered another woman in the premises of the compound. According to him, he just saw the woman walking along the road, shook her hand, and led her in. There, he murdered the victim and sucked her blood using his mouth. He then disposed of the body in the septic tank of the compound. When he told the police to check the tank, they found the woman's skeleton along with her purse and other personal belongings.

Unknown woman found near Gakere Road.

Onyancha murdered another woman in a lodging in Gakere Road, Nyeri, Kenya. He claimed that he lured a random woman he met on the street into the lodging house around midnight. He even negotiated with the employees of the place to mark down the price of the room. According to him, he did not sexually abuse the woman. All he did was strangle her to death and drink her blood. Onyancha left the corpse in the room and fled before daybreak.

- **Prostitutes**

Four prostitutes were murdered in different lodgings. Onyancha also targeted sex workers, and his modus operandi was to pretend that he was a client seeking their services. In other lodgings in Thika, he murdered four prostitutes, all on different occasions. Onyancha strangled them to death.

Hellen Nyambura

Nyambura was a prostitute that Onyancha invited to a lodging named Rwambogo Lodging. Onyancha invited the woman, rented a room in the said lodging house, and killed her with his bare hands. The morning after, Nyambura's body was found in the room they had occupied, and her death was all over newspapers and TV reports. However, Onyancha claimed that he was not even anxious because the evil spirits from his cult assured him that he would not be caught.

Jackline Wambui

After he murdered Nyambura, he then murdered Jackline Wambui, another prostitute in the Thika area. Her body was found in the Suitable Hotel, but the police had no leads on the suspect at that time.

- **Children**

Young Natan Baraza and an unknown female teenager While working as a security guard on a local flower farm, Onyancha killed a 9-year old boy, Natan Baraza, and a female teenager whose identity is unknown. Upon a search of the area, the police found the boy's and the girl's remains along with their belongings. Barraza's sandals were recovered in the area and his mother positively identified them. The boy's family was last seen watching a ball game near the flower farm. Months after his disappearance, a note was found in front of the farm, demanding almost a hundred thousand Kenyan Shillings in exchange for the boy's life.

Capture

In 2010, Onyancha was arrested when the police tracked the number he used to contact the family of another victim for ransom money. Upon his arrest, Onyancha confessed to the kidnapping crimes and the murder of 19 people. The man said that he was thankful that the police caught him - as it was his way of getting out of the curse of his cult and stopping the killing. These are the main things that he told the authorities:

He was recruited by his teacher to a blood-sucking cult back in 1996. He aimed to kill 100 people in 5 years to improve his position in the cult, but so far, he had only murdered 19. Onyancha stated that he did not meet any of the cult's members. The evil spirits governing the cult gave him the urge to kill and suck his victims' blood. These spirits would tell him when and where to kill, and the children and women victims were sacrificed to the evil ones. He admitted strangling them to death and drinking their blood after that. Onyancha, although under the 'instructions' of the evil spirits, developed a passion for killing and sucking his victims' blood. He only killed women and children since he viewed them as weak and vulnerable. He was happy to have confessed and was incredibly sorry for the murders he had committed. He stated that he was not himself when he killed and that he had already lost all power and influence over the evil spirits.

Onyancha led the police to all the areas where he dumped the bodies of his 19 victims. Although Onyancha admitted that he never sexually abused any of his victims, the psychologists suspect that he was not telling the truth since the mindset of a serial killer usually has a sexual component. Onyancha is still in custody and awaiting trial.

4. Albert Hamilton Fish: The Wolf of Wisteria

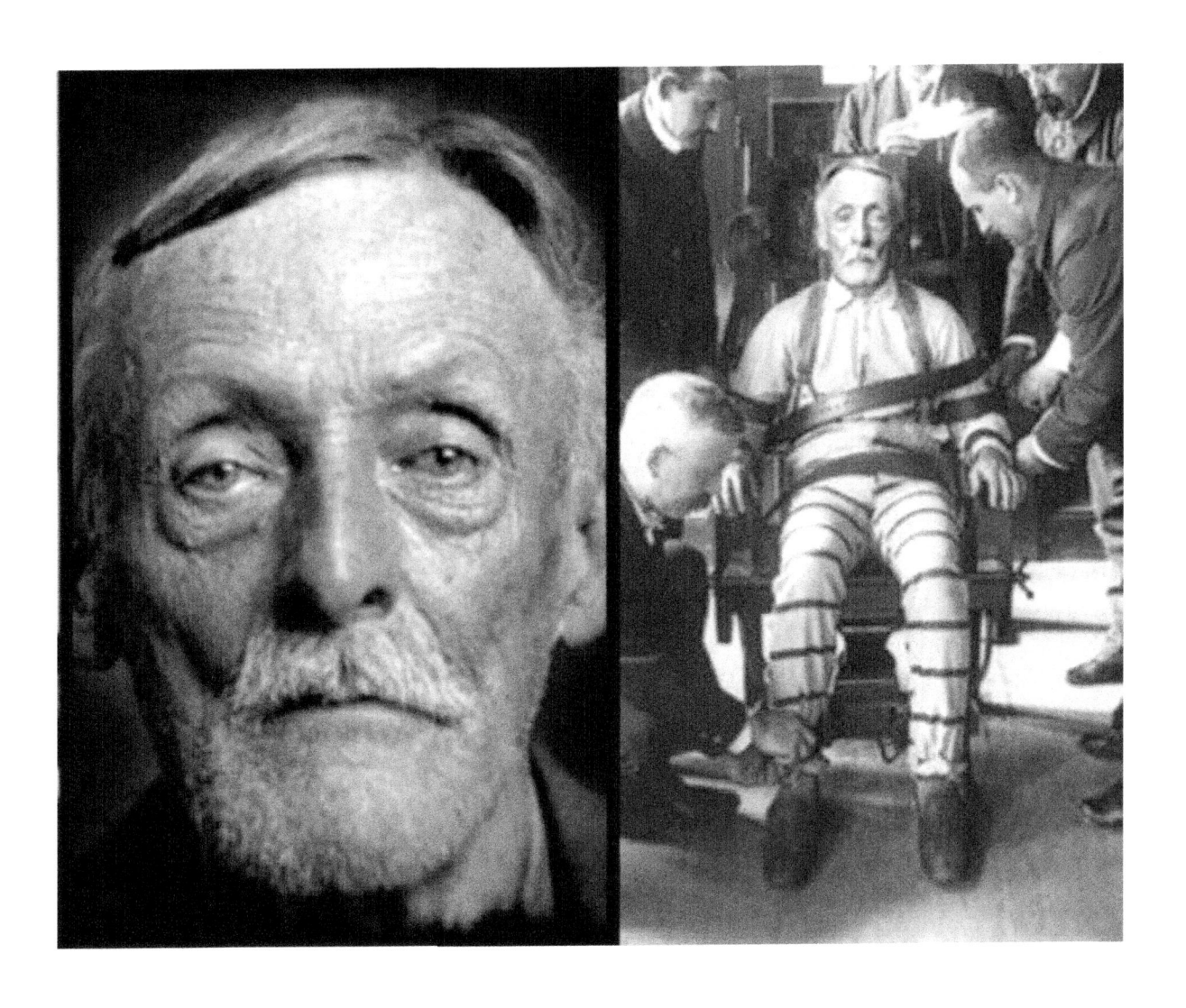

Albert Hamilton Fish was born on May, 19th 1870, and was electrocuted to death on January 16th, 1936, after being tried on multiple counts of murder, molestation, and cannibalism in the United States. He was known as the Werewolf of Wisteria and the Brooklyn Vampire in popular culture and urban legends. He was a prolific and perverted killer who was sexually driven to murder and perform lacerations upon the corpse. He claimed to have eaten and molested children in every state. Fish eventually confessed three murders to the police and admitted to having stabbed two victims during his interrogation.

Fish was born in Washington DC and grew up with three other siblings. His family had a history of mental illness. His siblings had been diagnosed with mental illnesses. His uncle had suffered from mania. Fish's mother would often experience aural or visual hallucinations. When Fish was a child, his father died of a heart attack, and his mother had to put the young boy in an orphanage. At the orphanage, Fish became a victim of abuse, trauma, and countless experiences that would affect him for the rest of his life. Fish was sexually abused at the orphanage and also experienced regular physical torture. The boys were often stripped naked and whipped by the orphanage management. During the nighttime, the boys would sexually abuse younger boys in the orphanage. Fish began to enjoy the pain he was subjected to. Perhaps his mental stability was shaken forever. It was too late when Fish's mother Ellen managed to secure a government job and take her son Hamilton out from the orphanage. When Hamilton Fish was twelve years of age, he was introduced to a telegraph boy in Washington. He started a sexually perverse relationship with the boy and practiced urolagnia (drinking urine) and coprophagia (eating feces). He used to frequent the town's public baths, where he would stand behind unnoticed and spied on boys while they took a bath. He felt sexually aroused by his voyeuristic adventures.

Adulthood and increasing psychopathic tendencies

As Fisher grew, his psychopathic and sick mentality also grew with him. In 1898, his mother arranged a marriage for him with a young woman, and the couple would go to have six children. At all points of time in his marriage, Fish was engaged in perverse sexual relationships with many people, primarily young boys. He worked as a prostitute and had started torturing some of his customers already. On one occasion, he took a nineteen-year-old boy named Thomas Kedden to a barn. Fish had a sexual relationship with him, but what awaited Thomas that fateful night was genuinely horrific. Fish took his partner to an abandoned farmhouse. After engaging in sexual acts with the boy, Fish tied him up and mutilated his penis. He cut off half of Kedden's penis with a razor blade as the boy screamed in vain. He had planned to kill Thomas after his sexual experiment and mutilation was complete, but it was summer season, and Fish worried that the stench of a corpse would emanate in the summer heat. Fish decided to sterilize the victim's mutilated penis with Vaseline and antiseptic, and after doctoring the wound, he left on a train and never heard from the boy again. Fish claimed that his fascination with the mutilation of genitals began with a trip he once took to the waxworks museum, where he saw a bisection of the human penis.

In 1917, Fish's wife left him, forcing him to raise his six children as a single father. He never engaged in physical abuse or sexual molestation with his kids but often encouraged them to spank his butt with a steel studded leather belt. Fish often prepared himself a dinner that would consist of solely raw meat. He sometimes gave his children the meat to eat so they could develop a taste for tough meat. This was also when his fascination with self-harm was rekindled, and he often practiced hitting himself with belts and steel studded nails in the behind until he would bleed. From 1917 to 1920, Fish's children reported him having recurring auditory and visual hallucinations. He was slowly losing his composure and sanity. At one point, he wrapped himself up in a carpet rug and started proclaiming that he was working on the orders of John the Apostle. Fish also inserted needles and metal pins in his groin and anus. This was something he would go on to do with many of his future child victims. After his arrest, he was examined medically, and his x-rays showed thirty metal pins stuck inside his abdomen. Fish was initially using the needles to pick the skin of his groin, but slowly he started inserting them to the point where he could no longer take them out.

In the years following 1919, Fish's condition worsened, and he became increasingly violent. He would target weak and helpless people who could hardly defend themselves from his attack. He had a carefully planned course of action. His victims were mostly children and handicapped or mentally challenged people. Fish also targeted African Americans because he felt that their absence would not get noticed easily since they were in the lower rungs of society.

During this time, Fish had assembled an arsenal of horrific weapons of torture, or what he liked to call the "Implements of Hell." Fish's "Implements of Hell" consisted of a butcher's knife, a meat cleaver, and a portable hand saw. Fish was suffering from full-blown psychosis during this time. He believed that he had experienced a divine revelation from God himself. He was divinely commissioned to killing, mutilating and sexually torturing children.

Grace Budd Murder

In 1928, Fish posed as Frank Howard and visited a young man named Edward Budd who had put up an ad offering his services in the country. Fish claimed to be a wealthy farm owner and offered Budd a job to work on his farm, secretly intending to mutilate the young boy and leave him bleeding to death. When he was at the residence of Budd, he saw his little sister,

Grace. Fish immediately became drawn towards the child. He abandoned his plans to castrate Edward Budd and instead began to devise a plan to mutilate the young girl's body. He had lavishly offered jobs not just to Edward Budd but also his friend Willie. The boys were excited at the handsome salary they had been offered by Fish, posing under the guise of farm owner Frank Howard.

Frank promised the Budds that he would return the next day and pick both of the boys up to start working on his farm. Before leaving, Howard offered little Grace to come along to his sister's niece's birthday party. He cajoled her parents that she could have some fun for a change. Grace put on her favorite coat and left with Frank Howard. When Grace's parents asked where he would take her, Fish gave them a fake address and promised to return her safely before nine in the evening.

Sadly, Grace would never return home again. That evening there was no word from Mr. Frank Howard.

Following a rather anxious and sleepless night, young Edward went to the police in the morning to officially report the missing of Grace Budd. Police soon revealed to the Budd family that it was a hoax all along. The address of Howard's sister, which he had given to Grace's parents, was fictitious. The old man was a fraud.

It was nearly June, and there was still no trace of Grace Budd or her body. It was as if she had disappeared from the face of the earth along with the strange old man. The police circulated thousands of posters of Mr. Howard along with a description given by Edward Budd and assigned more than twenty detectives to solve the case. After his arrest, Fish testified to his attorney that he had no intentions of raping Grace Budd but also admitted to having ejaculated twice while strangling the little girl.

Fish was charged with the murder and mutilation of Grace Budd. He admitted to having killed her and gave a spine-chilling account to add to his confession. He admitted taking Grace to an abandoned two storied building called 'The Wisteria Cottage' in the middle of a woody area. Fish asked Grace to look at the wildflowers growing outside the cottage while preparing his 'Implements of Hell.' After beheading the child, Fish undressed her and carefully chopped up pieces of her body with his butcher's knife. He packed parts of the meat in a newspaper which he took home to eat. He threw the remains of the body behind the stone walls of the Wisteria Cottage, which was recovered by the police after Fish's arrest. When Budd's family was called to identify the criminal, King was certain that they had caught the 'Boogey man' of Brooklyn.

Four-year-old Bill Gaffney was also kidnapped on February 11th, 1927, from the Brooklyn Trolley line. A motorman had seen an older man dragging away a crying boy who did not have a coat on. When Fish was asked about his relation to the incident, he confessed to having done unspeakable things to the boy. The

'Boogey Man' confessed to the police that he took Bill to the River Avenue dumping grounds. On the premises was an empty house, where Fish would keep the boy alive for the next day. He stripped Bill naked and tied his hands and feet. He gagged him so that he would not make any noise. Fish in the dumping ground burned bill's clothes and shoes.

Fish then proceeded to return to his home as if nothing had happened. The following noon Fish returned to the house in the River Avenue Dumps armed with his 'Implements of Hell.' Fish also made a heavy cat of nine tails at his home by cutting his leather belt into nine strips and fixing a short handle. The torture whip was about eight inches long. Fish whipped Bill's bottom with his improvised cat of nine tails until the child's bottom bled. He then cut the child's ears and nose with his razor blade. Bill's mouth was slit from his ear to ear. By this time, the child was dead. Fish then gouged out Bill's eyeballs and stuck a knife in his belly right below his belly button. Fish then put his mouth to the wound and drank as much blood as possible from the body. The cannibal killer then proceeded to cut the dead body carefully in pieces. The inedible pieces, such as the lower part of the child's limbs and the head, were collected in a gunny sack filled with heavy stones. Fish collected the other parts of the dead body that he would eat at his home. These pieces included the soft cartilage of the ears and the nose. Before leaving the scene, Fish took the gunny sack filled with Bill's remains and tossed it into the bottom of a slimy pool at the end of the road.

Fish further confessed to cooking the boy's body parts like the rear and genitals in his oven. He made a stew of his ears, nose and other cartilages along with celery, salt, pepper and spring onions. Fish prepared a rather elaborate dish of the boy's genitals and his bottom. He cut open the butt cheeks in two, slicing them with his sharp knife. Then he put strips of bacon and cheese on each butt cheek. The genitals were also washed and sliced, and added to the dish. The meat was then dressed in salt and pepper and placed in the oven for roasting. The meat was prodded with a wooden spoon at regular intervals to cook nice and even without charring. Fish claimed that the time to roast the child's rear was about two hours fully, and he consumed every bit of Gaffney's meat in about four days.

Fish was charged with a third count of homicide when he was convicted of murdering a fifteen-year-old girl named Mary O'Connor in the Far Rockaway. He had mauled and strangled the girl in a woody area close to where she lived. Mary's dead body was discovered by her family a day after Albert Fish murdered her.

Fish confessed to another murder of an eleven-year-old boy named Francis McDonald. He had picked up the child when he was playing catch with his friends in the Port Richmond neighborhood of Staten Island. The incident occurred in 1924, but it was only in March 1935, after being convicted of the murder of Grace

Budd that Albert Fish admitted to having murdered the eleven-year-old boy.

5. Joachim Kroll (The Ruhr Hunter)

Four-year-old Marion Ketter was missing, vanished from a playground in a suburb of Duisburg, Germany. The police had put men on the ground going door-to-door, making inquiries about the little girl. The morning of July 3, 1976, two officers entered a nondescript apartment block on Friesenstrasse. Almost immediately, they encountered the building supervisor, looking flustered. No, he hadn't seen the child, he said. He'd had his hands full, dealing with a blockage to the plumbing. Then, as the officers walked away to begin knocking on doors, he called them back. There was something he thought they might want to look into. Earlier that day, he'd asked a new tenant in the building, Joachim Kroll, if he knew what might be causing the blockage. "Guts," had been Kroll's calm reply.

Joachim Kroll was born in Hindenburg, Upper Silesia (now Zabrze, Poland) on April 17, 1933. His father was a coalminer, and Joachim was the youngest of eight children. A weakling as a boy, he had a bed-wetting problem that persisted into his teens. He was also considered mentally challenged, getting no further than Grade 3 in school and recording an IQ of 78.

During the war, Kroll's father was drafted into the German army, where he'd serve on the Eastern Front until his capture by the Russians. He would never return to his family. The rest of the Kroll clan escaped the newly communist east in 1947 and settled in North Rhine-Westphalia. Kroll spent his teen years here, growing up as a mommy's boy who was secretly obsessed with sex but at the same time terrified of approaching a girl. Instead, he became a chronic masturbator, a habit he would continue throughout his life. No doubt, he also developed rich fantasy life, a trait typical among serial killers.

In February 1955, Kroll's mother died. She had been his anchor, the center of his universe. Without her, Joachim became listless and deeply depressed. He began taking long walks, often at night, and it was during one of those excursions, he encountered 19-

year-old Inngard Strehl in the village of Walstedde. Typical of the disorganized serial killer, Kroll followed her on a whim, then pounced when she turned onto a darkened street. Inngard was strangled into submission and dragged to a barn. There, Kroll could eventually act out his sick fantasies on a living woman. The girl's body was discovered the next day, raped and strangled to death.

The murder of Inngard Strehl had whetted Kroll's appetite for more, but he was also fearful of being caught. Over the next year, he sated his carnal desires with inflatable sex dolls, but eventually, the lust for a living victim became nigh on impossible to resist. He went hunting again, luring 12-year-old Erika Schuletter to a field near Kirchhellen, where he raped and strangled her. After a cooling-off period of nearly three years, he struck again, stabbing Klara Jesmer to death in the woods near Rbeinhausen on June 17, 1959.

Joachim Kroll was not an intelligent man. But he possessed a criminal cunning and a strong sense of self-preservation. So far, he'd been careful to spread out his murders, both in terms of time and location. With his next murder, though, he'd add a perversion that would be difficult for the police to ignore. On July 26, 1959, he raped and murdered 16-year-old Manuela Knodt in a park near Bredeney, south of Essen. When Manuela's body was discovered, it was clear that several chunks of flesh had been sliced from her thighs and buttocks.

The same mutilations were found on the next victim, 13-year-old Petra Giese, whose body was discovered at Walsum on April 23, 1962. This time the killer had gone even further, slicing off both buttocks, along with the child's left forearm and right hand. Less than two months later, also in Walsum, 13-year-old Monica Tafel vanished on her way to school. She was found in a rye field, the now-familiar cuts made to her buttocks and thighs.

With the police now alerted to the presence of a cannibalistic serial killer, Kroll varied his M.O. with the next murder. When twelve-year-old Barbara Bruder was found at Burscheid in July 1962, her body bore no signs of mutilation. It is unclear whether Kroll deliberately left the body intact to throw the police off his trail or if he was disturbed before he could make his usual cuts. Either way, he promptly dropped out of sight after this latest murder and would remain so for the next three years. Then, in August 1965, the man known to police as the "Ruhr Hunter" was back.

Kroll often visited Lovers' Lanes during his nighttime excursions, hiding in the bushes and masturbating as he spied on young couples making out in their cars. On this particular evening, he spotted Hermann Schmitz and Marion Veen and, for some reason, decided to go beyond mere spying. Creeping up on the couple's Volkswagen, he punctured a tire, then backed off and hid in the bushes, waiting until they tried to drive off.

That brought the vehicle to a shuddering halt. As Hermann Schmitz got out to inspect the damage, Kroll crept up behind him and stabbed him several times in the back. He then turned his attention towards Marion Veen, but the quick-thinking young woman slid behind the wheel and drove off on the flat tire, leaving Kroll to skulk back into the bushes, frustrated at missing his prime target. By the time Marion returned with the police, Kroll was long gone, and Hermann Schmitz was dead. The murder was not initially linked to the Ruhr Hunter.

On September 13, 1966, Kroll raped and murdered Ursula Roling in Foersterbusch Park near Marl. Three months on, he struck again, raping five-year-old Ilona Harke before drowning her in a ditch near Wuppertal. When Ilona's body was found, there were steaks cut from her buttocks and shoulders.

Towards the end of 1967, Kroll moved to the village of Grafenhausen, where he lured 10-year-old Gabrielle Puetman to a field with the promise of showing her some rabbits. Instead, he produced a pack of pornographic pictures causing the girl to run off. By the time the police arrived to arrest him, Kroll had fled.

Perhaps frightened by that close call, Kroll took another of his long sabbaticals from murder, restraining himself for the next two years. When he did resume his murderous career in July 1969, the murder was atypical. Sixty-one-year-old Maria Hettgen was Kroll's oldest victim. She was found strangled to death in her home in Hueckeswagen. An autopsy would later reveal that she'd been raped and sodomized after death.

In May 1970, Kroll reverted to type, raping and strangling a child, 13-year-old Jutta Ranh, in Breitscheid. Thereafter followed his longest "cooling" period yet. It was six years before he waylaid 10-year-old Karin Toepfer on her way to school in Dinslaken Voerde. Like his previous victims, Karin was raped and strangled. Kroll's next move would be to the suburb of Laar, Duisburg, where he would commit his most heinous crime yet, the murder of Marion Ketter.

The police officers had been directed to the second floor by the super. Yet even as they climbed the stairs, they were certain that they were wasting their time. Surely, Kroll's offhanded quip about "Guts" had been some sick joke. There was only one way to find out. One of the officers rapped sharply on the door, then took a step back and waited. From within came the sound of shuffling footfalls.

The man who opened the door was short and stooped, with thick glasses and a bald pate. He had an imbecilic grin on his face and a hunched posture that made him look like a gnome in a Grimm fairy tale. The smell that wafted from the apartment was the not entirely pleasant aroma of something cooking. The officers could hear something bubbling furiously away on the stove. They'd hardly got out their question about the missing child when Kroll stepped aside and invited them in.

The apartment was small and cramped, and the cooking smells not quite disguising the unpleasant aroma of sweat and unwashed linen. An inflatable sex doll was arranged on the couch, and several others were scattered about the place. There were a number of battery-operated sex toys carelessly flung on tables and settees. An extensive collection of pornographic videotapes was piled high beside the TV. All of that faded into insignificance compared to what the officers found in the kitchen.

A tiny, eviscerated corpse lay half-concealed under the kitchen table, its hand crudely removed and chunks of flesh carved from the buttocks. On the stove, a stew of carrots and potatoes simmered, the child's missing hand bobbing in the thin gruel. In the fridge, pieces of human flesh were stored in plastic bags beside the milk and butter. A plumber would later flush a child's lungs and viscera from the drainage.

Taken into custody, Joachim Kroll appeared oblivious to the enormity of his crimes. He said he enjoyed rape and murder, so why shouldn't he be allowed to do it? Regarding cannibalism, he said that he'd initially cut flesh from his victims to save money on his grocery bills. However, he'd come to enjoy the taste of human flesh and preferred it now to any other meat.

At his trial in April 1982, Kroll said that he could remember 14 murders but that there might have been more. He seemed genuine to believe that he would walk away with no more than a slap on the wrist and stated that he was prepared to undergo an operation to cure his homicidal urges. Instead, he was found guilty on eight counts of murder and sentenced to life in prison.

Kroll would spend less than ten years behind bars. He died of a heart attack at Rheinbach Prison, near Bonn, on July 1, 1991.

6. Robin Gecht (Chicago Rippers Crew Leader)

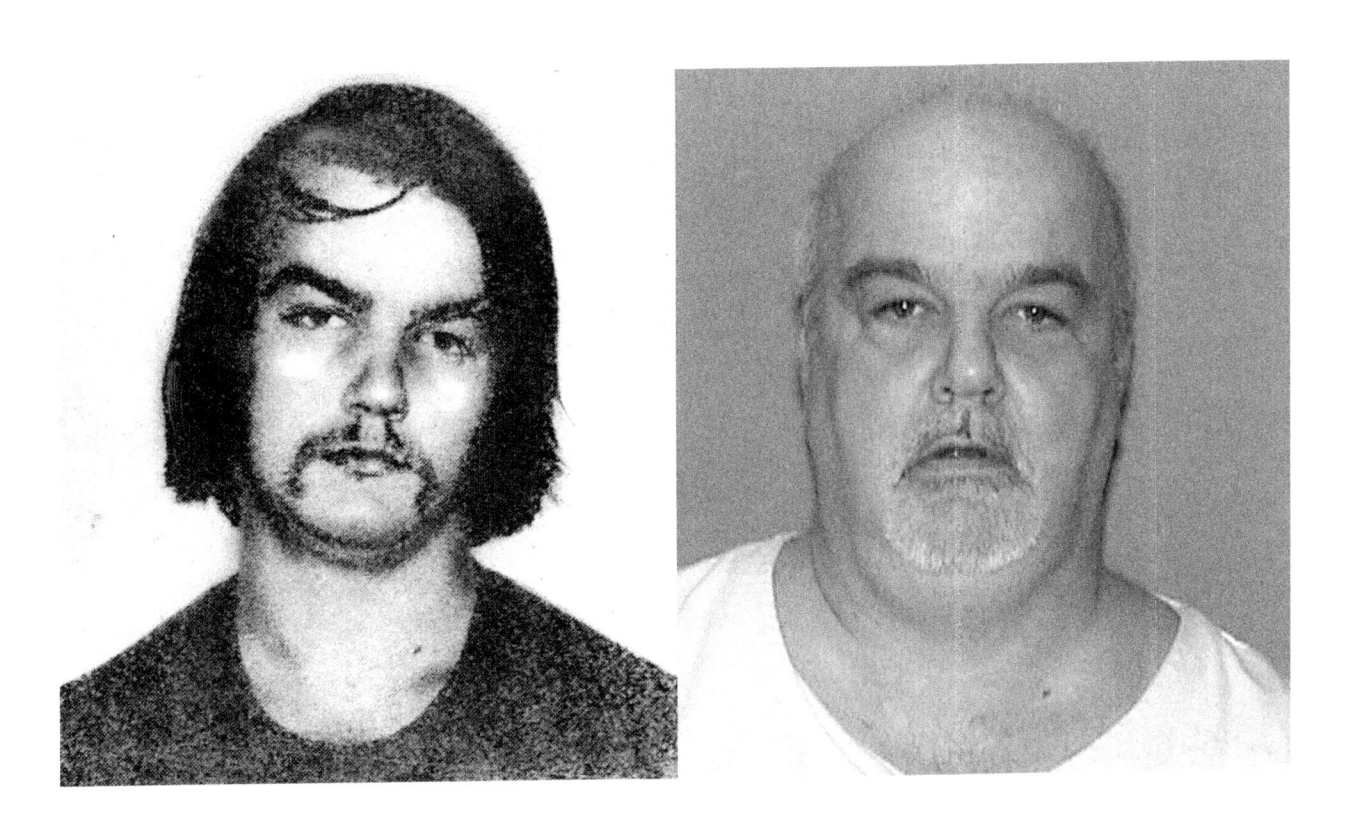

The Chicago Rippers Crew, comprising four people led by Robin Gecht, were the culprits in a string of female murders in Chicago, Illinois, from 1981-1982. Apparently, they picked women at random from their red van and raped and mutilated them. The gang cut their breasts using a piece of wire in a 'satanic ritual' while the leader read satanic bible verses. Gecht and the three other associates would mince the breast and eat it raw. To finally kill the victim, they would smash the woman's skull until her face was far from recognizable.

Robin Gecht was born on November 30, 1953, and he was a local of Chicago. In some reports, Gecht had a growing obsession with perverted things even when he was still a teenager. In fact, he molested his younger sister so many times that his parents sent him to live with his grandparents. As he grew older, Gecht became overly interested in Satanism, and he had different interpretations of bible verses. He also became a part-time employee of John Wayne Gacy, Jr,

Chicago's Killer Clown, who sexually abused and murdered about 30 men and hid their corpses in tunnels under his house. Gecht was one of the young teenagers that Gacy commissioned to dig the large tunnels, which Gecht didn't know how the latter would put into use. However, in some of the Killer Clown's murders, he stated that he was not in Chicago when they happened, and he assumed that his accomplices, one of them were Gecht, had performed the murders without his knowledge. Gecht, on the outside, was a charismatic and rather manipulative person. Women involved with him later claimed that they would have a good relationship at first until they discovered his strange sexual desires. Gecht would request his lovers to cut their nipples, stating that he wanted to know how they worked. Probably due to fear or even love, the women would obey and give him what he wanted. But, their pain would not end there. Gecht would explore the open wound and closely examine the severed nipples. This obsession led to the end of the relationship. Despite this, Gecht still managed to find a woman who would marry him. According to one of his associates, later in the couple's married life, Getch also cut off his own wife's nipples.

Chicago Rippers Crew Gecht, with his charisma and power over people, persuaded three people, Edward Spreitzer and the brothers Andrew and Thomas Kokoraleis, to join his cult that honored Satan. Like other satanic cults, the group was controlled by the leader, in this case, Gecht, who claimed to have contact with the devil. Together, they would perform sexual and gruesome acts on the women and their severed body parts.

In the string of murders, the group would go around town with their red van and pick a woman, usually aged between 20-30 years, at random. They would bind her and, in some cases, force her to take drugs. They would then rape, mutilate and strangle the victim to death. In every case, however, one of the victim's breasts was cut off. The usual causes of the victims' death were strangulation, bleeding through the large gaping wounds in their breast, and a smashed skull caused by an ax

In the later confessions of Thomas Kokoraleis, he detailed the rituals that they performed in Gecht's attic, a local motel, or their kidnapping van. Gecht decorated his attic with red and black inverted crosses and an altar with a red cross. The group would perform rituals at night when Gecht's wife went out to work. The severed breasts were taken to the attic, and each of the men would masturbate on the piece of flesh while their leader read Satanic Bible verses aloud. When everyone was done, Gecht would cut the breasts into smaller pieces and distribute them as a form of satanic communion, and they all would eat the chopped flesh raw. Then, Gecht would put all the severed breasts into a sort of a 'trophy box.' Spreitzer and the two Kokoraleis believed that these deeds were a form of sacrifice to Satan, and they were forced to obey Gecht in fear of what he may do to them since he had the 'power and communication" with the dark one.

Murders

The murders that the group committed between 1981-1982 accounted for 20 deaths of random women from Chicago. Their bodies were often found in graveyards, rivers, and abandoned places, usually undergoing advanced decomposition due to the large wounds from their open chests and breasts or smashed heads. The motive is believed to be ritualistic rather than theft because the victims' belongings and money were almost always intact.

Linda Sutton, a 28-year-old prostitute, went missing around May 1981. The Crew kidnapped her while she was walking the street. She was taken to a wooded area near the dumpsite and handcuffed. The men raped her and removed her breasts. They left her at the dumpsite. When a maid from a hotel in Villa Park reported smelling something awful in that part of the area, the owner called the police and found a woman's body in the field amongst the scattered garbage. The woman's body was in an advanced state of decomposition, but her estimated time of death was only three days ago. The experts believe that the corpse's condition was caused by the open wound of her breasts, giving parasites a large space to enter and rapidly cause her body to decay.

Lorraine Borowski; was an employee in a real estate office in Elmhurst, and she had been on her way to the office on May 15, 1982, when the crew offered her a ride. She refused, and two of the men grabbed her and dragged her inside. The gang took her to a motel, where they gang-raped her. She was bound, and a wire was placed around her breast. As the wire tightened, it slowly pierced through the woman's skin until the breast was finally cut off. According to Spreitzer, their leader was so aroused at the sight of the severed breast that he performed sexual acts on it. When Gecht was done with the breast, he smashed

Borowski's head in with an ax which instantly killed her. Borowski's body was found in a cemetery near the motel five months after her death. She was beyond recognition: her remains were almost completely decayed so that the cause of death could not be determined.

Rose Davis was a businesswoman who was walking to work in the middle of 1982. She was forced into the van by the crew, where they killed her with a small ax. Her body was found in a dark alleyway three months later, and it is believed that she tried to fight back. Dried blood was observed on her anus from the slashed internal organs, and her face was smashed from repeated strikes of an ax

Carole Pappas, the wife of a well-known player of the Chicago Cubs, was abducted while she was shopping in Wheaton, Illinois, on September 11, 1982. She was never seen alive again. Her remains were located five years later, and her death was ruled an accident.

Rafael Toradol; Hours after the attempted murder of Beverly Washington, one of the crew's victims, a drug dealer named Rafael Toradol, was killed. The crew allegedly shot the man and his companion.

Other murders

There were several other murders that Getch's followers confessed to in court. Spreitzer described the murder of two black prostitutes on different occasions. The first one was picked up by their van, taken to an alleyway where she was raped and removed her left breast with a knife. The other one was shot in the head and had her breast cut off. She was then handcuffed, chained, and thrown into a river with bowling balls to keep her weighed down. Some murders would be done by battering the victim's head in with an ax or a hammer. Gecht would force the three men to have sex with the wounds while the victim was still alive and screaming in agony. Other victims were tattered using a razor from head to toe.

Arrest

Three weeks after Washington's statement, the police stopped a red van, and sure enough, Edward Spreitzer was driving it. He told the police that the van belonged to Robin Gecht, and they raided his house. Washington's descriptions fit the image of Gecht, but the man denied all knowledge of the crimes. When he was first arrested, the police did not have enough evidence on Gecht to release him. However, Gecht, the two Kokoraleis, and Spreitzer were arrested after the authorities found out that they rented a room at the motel near the site where Linda Sutton's body was found.

Trial During the trial, Andrew and Thomas Kokoraleis and Edward Spreitzer confessed to being part of Robin Gecht's cult that killed women and cut off their breasts as a sacrifice for Satan. They admitted to performing rituals where they masturbated on severed breasts and ate them raw. They also confessed to participating in several murders of random women that they had picked in their van. However, their alleged leader, Robin Gecht insisted on his innocence and even denied that he was good friends with the three men. He remained tight-lipped all throughout and never admitted to any of the murders. Despite the eyewitness evidence, the authorities could not produce enough solid evidence of the murders against Gecht. So he was only sentenced to 120 years in prison for the attempted murder, rape, battery, and armed violence of Beverly Washington. Gecht was never charged with murder, and he will be eligible for parole in 2020. Meanwhile, the other members of the crew confessed to the crimes. Thomas Kokoraleis was given a life sentence for murder. His brother, Andrew Kokoraleis, was sentenced to death for the murder of Borowski, and he was the last man to be executed in Illinois on March 17, 1999. Edward Spreitzer was also given a death sentence, but his case was done after the moratorium for execution was enforced. He was charged for the murder of three women and the drug dealer and is to serve a lifelong sentence.

7.Karl Denke

Affectionately known as "papa" by his tenants, Karl Denke's arrest for attacking a man with an ax shocked his entire community. He had never shown any kind of aggression in his behavior before, and they did not believe it at first. Little did they know that this attack was the least surprising thing about their beloved landlord. A thorough search of his house revealed human flesh stored in large jars of curing salt. In a ledger, Denke had enlisted the names of the 40 people he had murdered and cannibalized over some time.

There is a scarcity of information about his early life, but there is enough information to piece out the fact that Denke was a dull child suspected to be retarded. He operated a rooming house and was a devout Christian who never missed a day at the church. His silent demeanor and his occasional philanthropy earned him the name "Papa Denke." His only source of income was the rent his tenants paid him.

The story of Denke's grisly life first came to light when he was charged for attacking a man named Vincenz

Oliver with an ax. When questioned by police, Denke claimed that he was defending himself against Oliver, believing him to be a burglar. After just two days of confinement, however, Denke hanged himself in his jail cell. A police team was then sent to his house to investigate the matter further. There, they found pieces of human flesh and bones preserved in a salt solution. Reports revealed that he dismembered and preserved his victims within a few hours of murdering them. There was also evidence of human flesh being cooked in cream sauce. More bones were found in his shed, from where the meat had been consumed and the bones cleaned. More than three hundred teeth were also discovered, where they were sorted according to size and preserved.

The Truth About Denke

Denke's method involved inviting beggars and vagabonds around the nearby train station to his home. He offered them shelter and food for a nominal cost at his rooming house. He would attack them with an ax once they were at his place and would later dismember their bodies into a number of smaller pieces. He enjoyed the taste of human flesh himself and also gave it to his tenants after cooking. There is also evidence suggesting that he used to sell human meat as pork in the nearby markets.

To this day, there is little known about his motives behind the murders and his cannibalistic behavior. One theory suggests that he did it out of desperation in order to have enough to eat. It was a time of recession in Germany, and starvation was prevalent. He had failed in his attempts at farming and market stocks. The result was a killing spree, after which he never lacked meat for food, even at the worst times. His neighbors believed him to have been consuming dog meat. Although forbidden, it was not that big of a deal for them. The case of Denke never garnered much attention from the public because of multiple factors. He had already killed himself in police custody, and reports of his cannibalism made it an uncomfortable topic of conversation.

There has been speculation as to the reason why Denke was never caught. It was later discovered that two of his previous victims had escaped after being hit with an ax. Surprisingly, the matter was not brought to the attention of the police. One possible explanation was his unsuspecting demeanor. Denke was perceived as being a dull and slow person who could have never committed such atrocities.

Furthermore, the allegations against him were brought up by beggars and vagabonds who weren't easily trusted. Denke's establishment provided cheap housing without asking his tenant's many questions. He depended on his reputation in the town to convince people to free him of the doubts and suspicion. The estimated 40 victims are based solely on the information contained in a ledger he maintained. His case is truly intriguing due to the lack of detailed information about his victims and his motives.

8.Albert Fentress (New York's Own Hannibal Lecter)

High school teacher Albert Fentress was a meticulous man, bordering, some would say, on obsessive-compulsive. The 35-year-old also appreciated the finer things in life. He dressed expensively, drove a Cadillac, and wore a Rolex watch, indulgences few in his profession could afford. Fentress, though was a diligent and savvy investor. In his financial affairs, as in everything else, he was a stickler for order and thoroughness. He'd never married and lived alone in a house kept spotlessly clean, both inside and out.

Fentress had two great passions in his life. The first was his profession. Graduating in the top percentile of his high school class in 1958, he'd gone on to obtain master's degrees in education and in his chosen subject, history. He was an unusual but highly regarded teacher. Often, he'd don period dress to get his point across to his students. For example, when teaching about World War Two, he liked to wear the garb of a Nazi officer, complete with a leather riding crop. These lessons, delivered in a quasi-German accent, were popular with the students. Some may have mocked Mr. Fentress behind his back, but no one ever dozed off in his classes.

The other pastime with which Albert Fentress occupied his time was stamp collecting. Fentress had few friends and rarely, if ever, socialized, so the solitary pursuit of philately took up a sizable chunk of his leisure time. The activity was perfectly suited to his fussy and scrupulous nature, but it was more than that. Ever the diligent investor, Fentress had acquired some valuable stamps over the years. His collection was worth a considerable amount of money. It, therefore, caused him great distress when, in the summer months of 1979, his house was burgled and his stamp albums stolen.

The police had no idea who might have broken into the Fentress homestead, but Albert Fentress thought that he did. Tuning into the school grapevine, he began to hear rumors that one of his students was responsible. Fentress was apoplectic. He went first to the school principal and then to the police, demanding action. The young man was questioned but denied taking the stamp albums. The police were forced to let the matter drop with no evidence to the contrary, which only served to infuriate Fentress further.

But Fentress wasn't the only one seething over the episode. Friends of the falsely accused youth were furious at the teacher's allegations. Over the following weeks, Albert Fentress arrived home several times to find his property vandalized, screens slashed, windows broken, and acid poured on his neatly trimmed lawn. On one occasion, someone urinated on his doorstep. Aggravated, Fentress applied for and obtained a gun permit. He then bought himself a revolver.

As July turned to August, the harassment of Albert Fentress by a person unknown continued. The teacher became increasingly paranoid, spending hours crouching in the dark, peering from behind drapes, hoping to catch some vandal in the act.

This obsessive behavior even began to creep into his dreams. On August 18, 1979, Fentress woke to find a notepad resting against his chest. This pad was usually stored in a drawer in his bedside table, and he had no recollection of taking it out during the night. Nonetheless, he had. Not only that, but he'd filled page after page with scrawled notes. As Fentress began reading, he became horrified by what he'd written. He had described, in great detail, the murder and dismemberment of a young man. Disgusted, he burned the notepad.

Two nights after that incident, Fentress was again at the window peering into his yard. As he was doing so, he thought that he saw a shape detach itself from the shadows. At first, Fentress thought that he might have imagined it, but then a young man stepped out from the cover of the trees and started walking across the lawn. In the moonlight, Fentress recognized him. He was Paul Masters, a senior at the school where Fentress taught.

Fentress had often played this scenario through in his mind. He usually waited until the vandal had done something incriminating in those rehearsals before apprehending him and calling the police. With Paul Masters in front of him, though, he acted differently. He walked calmly to the door, opened it, and called out to the boy.

Paul's first reaction was to back off, but Fentress reassured him that he meant no harm. He just wanted to talk. He then invited Paul inside, offering him a beer for his trouble. Accustomed to obeying instructions from a teacher, Paul complied.

No one but Albert Fentress knows what happened over the hours that followed. According to his later court testimony, he invited Paul Masters in, sat him down at the kitchen table, and served up the beer he'd promised. Then, as the youngster was distracted, he attacked and overpowered him and dragged him down to the cellar. There he bound the young man with ropes to a support beam. He then spent some time sexually assaulting Paul before shooting him in the head.

Fentress was now, according to his court testimony, operating in some sort of fugue state, entirely dissociated from the horrendous acts he was committing. With the young man slumped against his bonds, Fentress took a sharp knife and cut off his penis, which he carried upstairs, cooked, and ate. Afterward, he dragged Paul's body upstairs into his bedroom. Exhausted by his efforts, he collapsed on the bed and fell asleep.

When he awakening the next morning, Fentress was horrified to find the mutilated and bloody corpse beside him. Yet, he had no immediate recollection of what had happened. The sensation, he said, was similar to what he'd experienced two days earlier. And then it struck him. He had acted out the exact scenario that he'd written about in his notebook. Horrified, Fentress called a friend and told him about the murder. The friend, at Fentress's behest, called the police. Fentress was arrested.

A year of legal wrangling went by before Albert Fentress was eventually put on trial and found not guilty by reason of insanity. He was sent to the Pilgrim Psychiatric Center, diagnosed with narcissistic personality disorder, obsessive-compulsive disorder, and dissociative fugues. He responded well to treatment and was soon using his teaching skills to tutor other inmates and even the facility staff.

In 1999, a Suffolk County jury decided that Fentress was no longer a danger to society and recommended his release. However, Fentress's joy at the prospect of his imminent freedom was short-lived. The State Supreme Court set aside the verdict and ordered that Fentress, who had been described in the media as "New York's Own Hannibal Lecter," must remain locked up.

In 2006, Fentress tried again, but his appeal backfired when the State produced two former students of Poughkeepsie Middle School. They testified that Fentress had sexually molested them in the months preceding the murder of Paul Masters. The judge then ordered Fentress to be moved to a more secure facility at the Mid-Hudson Psychiatric Center in Goshen, New York.

9. Jose Luis Calva Zepeda (The Cannibal Poet)

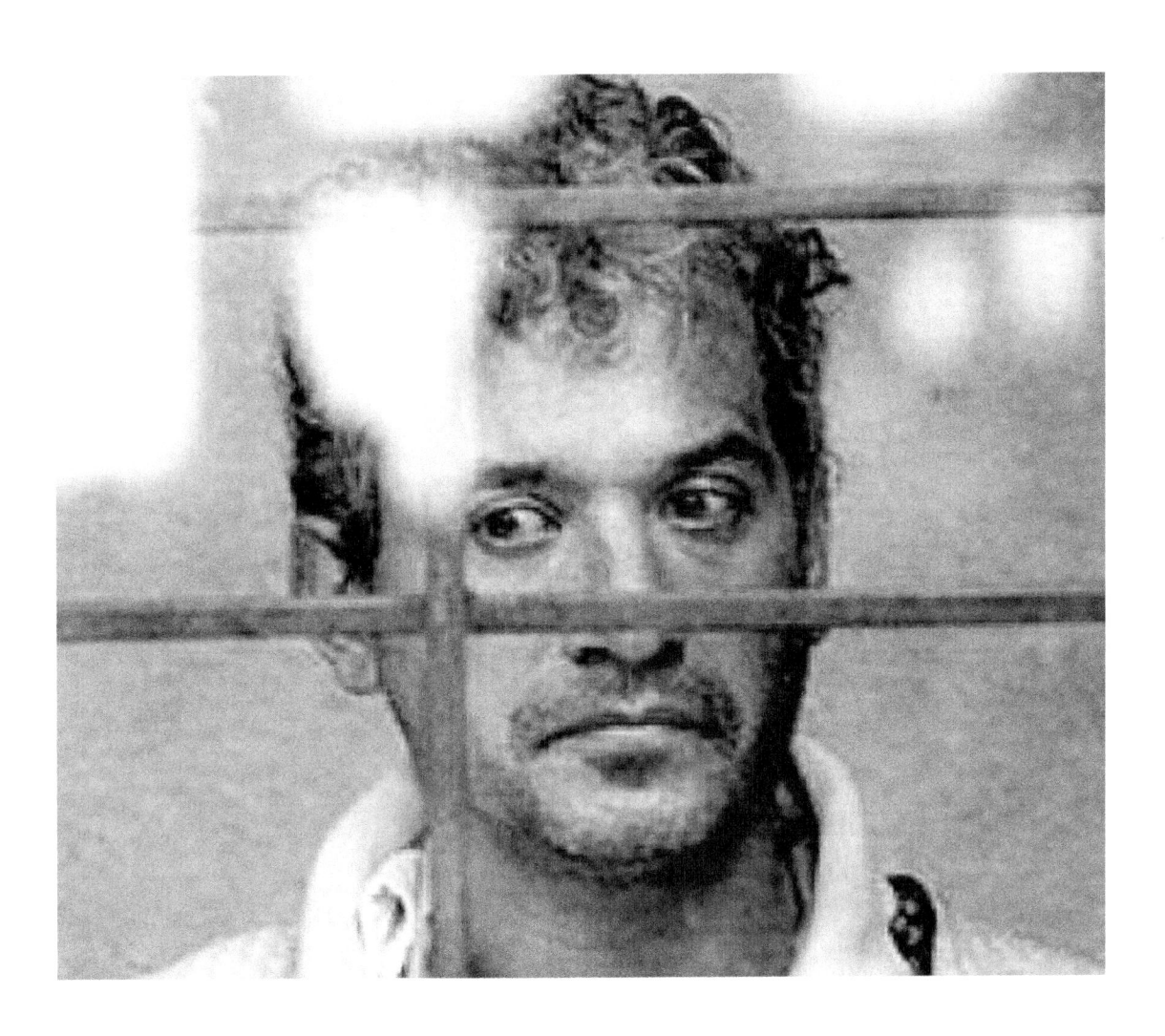

Alejandra Galeana had been missing for three days when her mother, Soledad, contacted the police. She had a lead on her daughter's whereabouts. Neighbors had seen Alejandra, she said, entering the Mexico City apartment of her ex-boyfriend, José Luis Calva Zepeda.

At first, the officers were disinclined to follow up on the tip. Soledad Fernandez sounded hysterical, especially when she launched into a tirade about Calva Zepeda. She'd never liked the man, she said. He was creepy and far too full of himself. He said he was a poet, a playwright, a movie director, and a singer. He said he earned $200 a day in royalties from some books he'd written, but his clothes, cheap and well-worn, belied that fact. Then Soledad said something that finally got the police's attention. Since the breakup, Zepeda had been harassing Alejandra, threatening to kill her and commit suicide if she didn't return to him. With probable cause established, the officers decided to visit Zepeda. They could hardly have known that they were about to uncover one of the most sensational cases of cannibalism in Mexico's history.

Jose Luis Calva Zepeda was born on June 20, 1969, in Mexico City, Mexico. His father, Esteban, died when Jose was just two years old. After that, the boy suffered physical and psychological abuse at the hands of his mother, who brought home a succession of live-in lovers and forced Jose to call each of them "Dad." At the age of seven, he was raped by a 16-year-old friend of his older brother. Soon after, he ran away from home. Although he later returned, he began spending much of his time on the streets, begging, committing petty thievery, and prostituting himself to pedophiles.

Despite that inauspicious start to life, Jose was a bright boy who showed a particular aptitude for language and enjoyed reading and writing. At a young age, he was already crafting his own short stories and poems. And he was already showing signs of the narcissist he'd later become, constantly boasting to his schoolmates that he was going to be a famous author and playwright.

Zepeda was 27 when he married in 1996. The union would produce two daughters before it ended in divorce seven years later. After that, Zepeda's ex-wife absconded to the United States, taking the children with her. Thrown into deep despair by the breakup, Zepeda lost himself in his writing, producing works that were dark, macabre, and menacing, with titles like "Requiem for a Lost Soul," and tellingly, "Cannibal Instincts."

Jose Calva Zepeda was by now in his mid-thirties, a prematurely gray but handsome man with a good line of talk that seldom failed to impress the ladies (at least until they realized the deep insecurity that lies beneath his boasts). In 2004, an attractive young pharmacist named Veronica Consuelo Martinez Casarrubia fell for his charms. The couple began a relationship over the protests of Veronica's mother, who warned her daughter that there was "something not right" about Zepeda.

Those fears were realized when Veronica disappeared in April 2004, shortly after breaking off her relationship with Zepeda. Her dismembered remains were discovered in the state of Chimalhaucan on April 30. So crudely was the body hacked apart that a detective was heard to comment that it looked as if a combine harvester had run over her.

Calva Zepeda was the obvious suspect, but he'd gone to the ground, and an extensive search failed to find him. He was, in fact, hiding in plain sight, taking an apartment close to the famed Plaza Garibaldi in central Mexico City. He was still at large in April 2007, when the mutilated corpse of a prostitute known as "La Jarochan" was found in Tlatelolco. Zepeda has since been named as her likely killer.

Not long after that discovery, Zepeda began dating Alejandra Galeana.

On October 8, 2007, police officers arrived at Calva Zepeda's building to enquire after Alejandra's whereabouts. The concierge confirmed that Zepeda was home, but there was no reply when officers knocked at his door. They decided to force the lock, busting in on a scene that sent seasoned detectives scuttling out to throw up in the corridor.

On the stove, set a frying pan with chunks of flesh cooling in a thin gruel. Wedges of lime were arranged to the side, obviously intended as a seasoning for the cutlets. In the refrigerator, the police found a leg and part of an arm, both de-boned. The bones were later found stuffed into a cereal box.

An even more gruesome discovery awaited in the bedroom. Alejandra's rotting, mutilated corpse was found crammed into a closet, chunks of flesh hacked from her arms, legs, and buttocks.

As the detectives continued their search, word came that Calva had been captured. When the police had knocked on his door, he'd climbed out of the window of his top-floor apartment and had tried to escape by jumping from one balcony to the next. Losing his grip, he'd fallen, suffering head injuries in the process.

Zepeda was taken to hospital while the search of his apartment continued. It yielded an array of sick artifacts, a collection of knives and machetes; books on witchcraft and sadism; his writings, poems, horror novels, and screenplays, including the aforementioned "Cannibal Instincts"; a collection of animal porn videos.

Meanwhile, Zepeda had made enough of a recovery to face police questioning. He admitted to murdering Alejandra but insisted he'd killed her while high on booze and cocaine. He denied cannibalizing the corpse. The mutilations were merely in order to dispose of the body, he said. Why then had he been cooking chunks of flesh when the police arrived? According to Zepeda, his intention was to feed the meat to stray dogs in the neighborhood. The police did not believe him. Why would he skin the flesh and season it with lime if that was what he planned to do?

Jose Luis Calva Zepeda was eventually arraigned on two counts of murder. However, he would never see the inside of a courtroom. On December 11, 2007, he was found in his prison cell, hanging by a makeshift noose fashioned from his belt. The prolific writer had left behind no suicide note.

10. Alexander Spesivtsev

Better known as the "Siberian Ripper," Alexander Nikolayevich Spesivtsev lived in the Siberian town of Novokuznetsk with his mother, Lyudmila. From 1991 to 1996, he murdered and cannibalized more than 80 victims, out of which he confessed to committing 19 of them, and was only convicted for four murders. His victims were mostly street children from the less fortunate section of society.

He was born in 1970 in a disturbed household. He was tortured and beaten by his father as a child. His only support was his mother, with whom he had an unusual relationship. His mother would tell him stories of murder at bedtime and show him pictures of corpses from a very early age. He soon got accustomed to violence and developed sadistic tendencies. He committed his first murder at the young age of 18, after which he was admitted to a mental hospital. But he was released shortly after. He moved into an apartment with his mother and a Doberman, where together they lured in and murdered several victims.

His mother would lure children into their house, promising them food, clothes, and shelter. Once they had been lured in, Spesivtsev stabbed them from behind. He did not kill his victims swiftly, rather he watched them bleed to death from the multiple stab wounds he had inflicted on them.

Despite several complaints of a rotten smell around Alexander's apartment and the loud rock music played in his house all throughout the day, the police continued to ignore the matter. They thought it was a simple case of a die-hard rock fan living in unhygienic conditions. There were, however, no complaints from his neighbors regarding the disappearance of street kids, and none of them suspected that a murderer was amongst them.

When police discovered a dismembered body part floating in the river, they investigated the possibility of a serial killer on the loose. At this point, police finally paid some attention to the complaints of stench around Alexander's house. The authorities found blood splattered all over the walls, floors, and even the ceiling. The entire house was scattered with dead remains of multiple victims, with human flesh stuck to the utensils. A rib cage lay on the floor in the living room, and the bathroom had a headless corpse in it.

A fifteen-year-old Olga Galtseva was found in his house in a battered and mutilated state. She died on the way to the hospital after telling the police about the incident. Lyudmila asked her and a couple of her friends to carry some bags inside the house. They were ambushed by Alexander as soon as they entered, where he raped all of them. He killed one of the girls after sexually abusing her for quite a while and made the other two girls cut up her body. His Doberman killed the second girl while his mother cooked the cut-up corpse of the first one. They fed on the meat and force-fed Olga the dead remains of her friend before stabbing her repeatedly.

The police soon arrested Alexander and Lyudmila. There he admitted his guilt while his mother denied any involvement. However, they were both booked as murderer and accomplice and were sentenced to life imprisonment on trial. The motive for the murders, as stated by him during the trial, was to clean the world of the "filth" that those poor children represented. He blamed Russia's democracy and negligence for the widespread poverty prevalent in the country. He hated the country for not paying attention to the state of its citizens and killed the children who were to him a constant reminder of the country's plight. Even if he could justify his brutal murders as an attack on the state of the nation, he could not explain his acts of sexual abuse and cannibalism against his victims. While his mother did not kill any of the victims, she was the one who lured, cut up, and cooked the bodies. Although Alexander was found to be mentally ill during the course of the trial, his mother was assessed to be just fine. She refused to comment on the motives, but it was speculated that a history of domestic abuse at the hands of her husband made her prone to cold-blooded violence. Whether her involvement in the crime was forced or of her own will remains unknown to this day

11. Alfred G. Packer (The Colorado Cannibal)

When we think of the Old West, our minds are drawn inexorably to the vision painted for us by Hollywood, of desperadoes, cattlemen, Indian fighters and wagon trains, of heroism and adventure. But the West had a dark side too. Many of the famous gunfighters, both outlaws and lawmen, were cold-blooded psychopaths and would probably have been classed as serial killers in the modern era. And there are tales untold of rape and murder, pillage and plunder, not to mention genocide and the near extermination of the buffalo. Within that tainted history, one also finds stories of cannibalism, of mountain men like John Garrison Johnson and Boone Helm, of the doomed Donner party, and, of course, the most notorious Western cannibal of them all, Alfred G. Packer.

Packer was born in Allegheny County, Pennsylvania, on November 21, 1842. As a young man, he worked as a cobbler, but he enlisted in the Union Army with the outbreak of the Civil War. Accepted for duty on April 22, 1862, he was honorably discharged just seven months later when it was discovered that he had epilepsy. He then made his way west, intent on making his fortune in the Colorado goldmines.

In late 1873, the 31-year-old Packer was hired by some 20 prospectors to guide them from Bingham Canyon, Utah, to the goldfields in Colorado's the San Juan Mountains. The party set off in November 1873 but was soon in trouble when they lost most of their supplies during a river crossing. Nonetheless, they struggled on and eventually made it to the Ute camp near Montrose, arriving in January 1874.

They were given food and shelter there, and Chief Ouray strongly advised them to stay and see out the winter. Most agreed, but a small group of prospectors - Shannon Wilson Bell, Israel Swan, James Humphrey, Frank Miller, and George "California" Noon – were keen to reach the goldfields. The distance that had to cover was just 40 miles, and despite the weather, they were certain they could make it. After persuading Alfred Packer to continue as their guide, they departed the camp on February 9. Unfortunately for them, their information was wrong. The fields were 75 miles away, not 40.

Two months later, on April 16, Albert Packer walked out of the woods at the Los Piños Indian Agency on Cochetopa Creek near Saguache. He seemed quite healthy for a man who claimed to have wintered in the wilderness and was well funded, drawing bills from several wallets to pay whiskey at the saloon. Asked about the whereabouts of his companions, Packer appeared confused. They'd gone on ahead of him, he said, as he'd hurt his leg and had fallen behind.

But the other prospectors had not made it into town, and the more the saloon patrons listened to Packer's story, the more they became convinced that he had killed and robbed his companions. Packer denied this outright. He kept up those denials even after an Indian scout found chunks of human flesh along with the trial he claimed to have walked.

On May 8, 1874, a month after he'd emerged from the wilderness, Packer appeared at the office of camp commander General Charles Adams. Somewhat the worse for a drink, he told the general that he wanted to come clean about what had really happened out there in the wilderness. He then launched into a rambling confession of sorts.

According to Packer's account, the party had become lost and had run out of supplies. As the conditions worsened, Israel Swan, the oldest of the group at 65, had died. The others, desperately hungry and unable to see another way out of their predicament, decided to eat him. Four days later, James Humphrey had died and was also eaten. Packer admitted to taking $133 from Humphrey's wallet as "he wasn't going to need it any longer."

The third to go was Frank Miller, who died in some kind of "accident." Packer didn't elaborate on what the accident was. According to him, he'd been out collecting firewood when it happened. Packer wasn't present either when George Noon died. He'd been out hunting for several days, he said. When he returned, he found that Shannon Bell had shot Noon. That left just Packer and Bell alive, and by Packer's account, Bell had by now gone crazy. He'd attacked Packer the minute he'd walked into the camp. Forced to defend himself, Packer had killed the madman.

Packer's story sounded feasible, but to prove its veracity, the bodies needed to be recovered. A search party was therefore dispatched, with Packer acting as a guide. They found nothing, leading them to suspect that Packer had deliberately led them away from evidence that might have incriminated him. On the search party's return, Packer was arrested and placed in the jailhouse at Saguache on suspicion of murder.

Packer was still in the jailhouse in August 1874 when a man named John A. Randolph, an artist working for Harper's Weekly Magazine, came across a cluster of five bodies near Slumgullion Pass. Randolph got out his pad and pencils, sketched the scene, then hurried to Saguache to report his find.

Realizing that these must be the missing prospectors, Hinsdale County coroner W. F. Ryan assembled a posse of twenty men and set out for the site. When they arrived, it was immediately clear that Packer's story had been a lie. The bodies were close together, not scattered along the trail as he'd described. It was also apparent that there had been postmortem mutilations to the corpses. One was missing a head; others had chunks of flesh hacked from them. One appeared to have put up a fight.

But were these the missing prospectors? A member of the original search party was found and identified each of them. By process of elimination, it was determined that the headless corpse was Frank Miller. The bodies were buried on a bluff overlooking the scene of their demise, an area known today as "Dead Man's Gulch."

Having completed the burials, the party left for Saguache, intent on confronting Alfred Packer's obvious lies. They arrived to find that he'd escaped the jailhouse and fled. He would remain at large for nine years.

In March 1883, a man named Frenchy Cabizon walked into a saloon in Fort Fetterman, Wyoming. Cabazon had been a member of the original prospecting party out of Utah, so he recognized the booming laugh from the other side of the room. It was Alfred Packer, or as he was calling himself these days, John Schwartze.

Packer was arrested on the spot. Hauled before a grand jury in March 1883, he was indicted on five counts of murder. Locked in the jailhouse, Packer felt another prickling of conscience and asked to speak to General Adams to make his "confession."

Packer's new account had the party running into a severe snowstorm days after leaving Chief Ouray's camp. By day ten, they were helplessly lost, out of provisions and surviving on pine gum. Some in the party, especially Shannon Bell, were being driven to madness by their hunger.

Packer was the official scout of the group, so Israel Swan asked him to climb to the top of a nearby peak to see if he could find a way through the blizzard. Packer did as he was asked but was unable to find a route. When he returned to the camp days later, he found Shannon Bell squatting by the fire, roasting a large chunk of meat. Nearby lay the corpse of Frank Miller, and it was obvious where the meat had come from. The other three men were lying close by; their heads caved in by blows from a hatchet.

As Packer approached the fire, Bell picked up the bloody hatchet and attacked him. Packer fired his rifle, hitting Bell in the stomach. Then, as Bell slumped to the ground, Packer snatched the hatchet away and struck him on the head.

Over the days that followed, Packer tried several times to leave the camp, but each time was driven back by fresh snow flurries. Eventually, driven by his desperate hunger, he ate some of the flesh that Bell had carved from the corpses. He managed to survive this way for two months until the snow thawed, and he could make his way. He admitted taking money from the dead men, but only because they'd have no further use for it, and it was pointless leaving it behind.

Alfred Packer went on trial on April 6, 1883, at the Hinsdale County Courthouse in Lake City, Colorado. The indictment was for one charge of murder only, that of Israel Swan. Testifying in his own defense, Packer stuck steadfastly to his story, refusing to budge even when the prosecutor caught him out in one lie after another. Unsurprisingly, he was found guilty of murder.

One of the legends that have sprung up around the case regards the words used by Judge Melville B. Gerry in delivering his judgment. A popular and widely believed version goes something like this: "Alfred Packer, you voracious man-eating son of a bitch, there was only seven registered Democrats in Hinsdale County, and you've gone and eaten five of them. I sentence you to be hanged by the neck until you are dead, dead, dead. I would sentence you to hell if I could, but the statutes forbid it."

In truth, Judge Gerry said nothing of the sort. He did, however, sentence Alfred Packer to death. The date set for Packer's execution was May 19, 1883, but in another twist to this already convoluted case, the judgment was thrown out on a technicality. At the time that Packer committed his crimes, Colorado had not yet attained statehood. It was therefore determined that the newly incorporated State of Colorado could not try Packer for murder. A new trial was ordered. The charge now was five counts of voluntary manslaughter. Found guilty, Alfred Packer was sentenced to 40 years in jail, eight years for each of his five victims.

Packer would serve 16 years in prison before being paroled in 1901 on medical grounds. He moved to Deer Creek Canyon, Colorado, where he spent the last five years of his life regaling the local children with his tales of adventure. He died on April 24, 1907. During his final years, the infamous Colorado Cannibal ate no meat.

12. Andrei Chikatilo (The Red Ripper)

Lena Zakotnova scanned the crowd milling around the tram station. It was December 22, 1978, a frigid, overcast day in Shakhty, southern Russia, but Lena didn't mind. She was bundled up against the cold in her new red coat. The nine-year-old was focused entirely on the crowd, trying to pick out the kindly older man she'd met yesterday. He'd promised her some imported chewing gum when he saw her again. Now she spotted him, a tall, gray-haired man of about forty, slightly balding and with overlarge spectacles perched on his nose. Lena waved excitedly, drawing his attention. The man gave her a placid smile and began weaving his way through the throng.

Lena had hoped that the man would have the candy with him, but he didn't. He said that he'd forgotten it at home. Noting her disappointment, he smiled sympathetically. Then an idea seemed to occur to him. His house was only a short distance from the tram stop. Would she like to walk there with him to fetch the chewing gum? Disregarding all of her mother's stern warnings about trusting strangers, Lena nodded eagerly. The man held out his hand, and Lena took it.

Andrei Chikatilo had never killed anyone before that gloomy winter's day in 1978. But he'd dreamed about it many times, playing the scenario over and over in his head. Now, as he approached the rundown shack that he rented on the banks of the Grushevka River, he did a furtive scan of the area. No one had seen him and the girl approach the lean-to. Good. Barely able to contain his excitement, he led Lena up the rickety stairs, fished a key from his pocket, and turned it in the lock.

Lena's disappearance was reported to the police that afternoon. The following day, her body washed up downstream, and the missing person case became a murder inquiry. Then the police had a break; a tram passenger came forward and reported that she'd seen Lena walking hand-in-hand with an older man. The description provided by the witness was (in hindsight) remarkably accurate, but the police appeared to disregard it. Instead, they arrested a known sex offender named Alexsandr Kravchenko, a man who bore no resemblance to the witness statement. Kravchenko would eventually be tried, found guilty, and executed for the murder of Lena Zakotnova. Andrei Chikatilo, meanwhile, remained free. He would go on to become the most brutal and prolific serial killer in Russian history.

Andrei Romanovich Chikatilo entered the world in the village of Yablochnoye, Ukraine, on October 6, 1936. Born amid Stalin's ill-fated land reform policies, he was familiar with hardship from an early age. It was an era when many desperate people were forced to resort to cannibalism in order to survive. In fact, according to Chikatilo's mother, his older brother Stephan had been waylaid by some of their neighbors, killed and eaten. Whether the story was true or not, it had a profound effect on young Andrei.

Chikatilo was an intelligent boy who preferred reading books to playing with friends. His slightly effeminate demeanor made him an easy target for bullies. He was also a chronic bed-wetter, a habit that earned him regular beatings.

By the time he reached his teens, Chikatilo was a tall, gangly individual editor of the school newspaper and the student body's "political information officer." Those positions earned him some kudos from his fellow students and at least stopped the bullying, but he was still painfully shy, especially around females.

At 18, Chikatilo applied to Moscow University to study law but failed the entrance exam. By then, he'd attempted many sexual liaisons with women, all of them ending in humiliation when he failed to maintain an erection. He tried to force himself on a woman during his compulsory military service, but she fought him off. Chikatilo, though, was not disappointed. During the struggle, he had become aroused and ejaculated. It was the first time he realized that violence was more exciting to him than sex.

After completing his national service, Chikatilo moved to the small town of Rodionovo-Nesvetayevsky, just north of Rostov, where he found work as a telephone engineer. While living there, Chikatilo's sister introduced him to a woman named Fayina, who became his wife and later bore him two children. Seeking a better life for his family, Chikatilo enrolled in a correspondence course with Rostov Liberal Arts University. In 1971, he gained a degree in Russian Literature, a qualification that enabled him to find a position as a teacher at Vocational school No. 32 in Novoshakhtinsk.

Chikatilo was poor at his new vocation, lacking the necessary authority to control his students. He did, however, acquire a reputation for sexual harassment. In one notable instance, he was beaten up by a group of students after he was caught fondling a sleeping child in a boys' dormitory. That incident led to

Chikatilo being fired, and over the years that followed, he flitted from one teaching job to another, moving on whenever a new scandal arose.

In 1978, Chikatilo moved his family to Shakhty, where he committed his first murder. Thereafter, he appears to have restrained his murderous urges until 1981. That was also the year that he lost his teaching job and was unable to find another. Desperate, he accepted a position as a supply clerk at a local industrial complex, a job that involved travel to different parts of the Soviet Union. Soon Andrei Chikatilo would take his murderous show on the road.

On September 3, 1981, almost three years since he'd killed Lena Zakotnova, Chikatilo claimed a second victim. Larisa Tkachenko was 17 years old when she met Andrei Chikatilo at a bus stop outside the Rostov library. Chikatilo offered to buy her a meal, and some drinks in exchange for sex and Larisa agreed. However, she had second thoughts once he led her into the woods. She tried to flee, but he caught her and beat her into submission, and then suffocated her by forcing dirt and leaves down her throat. He then committed his first known act of cannibalism, biting off one of his victim's nipples and swallowing it. As a final indignity, he masturbated over the corpse before covering it with branches.

According to Chikatilo's later confession, the murder of Larisa Tkachenko "elated" him and left him eager to repeat the act. Over the next year, he claimed seven more victims, five females, and two young males. He then went to the ground for six months before re-emerging on June 18, 1983, to slaughter 15-year-old Laura Sarkisyan. Before the summer was over, he'd claimed three more victims. Lyuda Kutsyuba, 24, an unidentified woman aged between 18 and 25 and a seven-year-old boy, Igor Gudkov.

By September 1983, the so-called "Forest Strip killings" were causing alarm in Moscow. The Soviet authorities had always denied the presence of serial killers in their country, but 14 mutilated and partially cannibalized corpses were impossible to ignore. One of the country's best investigators, Major Mikhail Fetisov, was asked to look into it. He, in turn, assembled a team of crack investigators led by the brilliant forensic analyst Victor Burakov.

Burakov quickly determined that the murders had their epicenter in Rostov. Setting up his headquarters there, he dispatched his team to question every known sex offender in the area. One of those interviewed was Andrei Chikatilo, although he was quickly dismissed as a suspect because his blood was type A. Semen found at the crime scenes had led investigators to believe that their killer was type AB.

A year passed, during which Chikatilo claimed 15 more victims, and the task force got no closer to catching him. In desperation, Burakov asked Rostov Medical Institute psychiatrist, Aleksandr Bukhanovsky, to compile a profile of the "Forest Strip

Killer," the first time this methodology had been used in a Soviet criminal investigation.

But a profile wasn't going to catch the Forest Strip Killer. That would require serious legwork. Burakov had by now established that the elusive murderer often picked his victims from transport hubs. He, therefore, dispatched men to patrol the bus, tram, and train stations.

On the first day of the surveillance, a detective named Aleksandr Zanosovsky spotted a tall, balding, middle-aged man with glasses wandering through the crowd. The man was acting suspiciously, so Zanosovsky approached and asked for his papers. The documents appeared in order, identifying the man as Andrei Chikatilo.

Several weeks later, Zanosovsky spotted the same man and decided to follow him. Over the next several hours, he kept Chikatilo under surveillance, watching as he visited tram hubs and bus stations. At each location,

Chikatilo approached random females and tried to talk to them. If a woman rebuffed him, he simply shrugged his shoulders and moved on to someone else. At one point, he attempted to fondle an intoxicated young woman and got a mouthful of abuse for his trouble. Using that as a pretext, Zanosovsky moved in and arrested him.

Chikatilo appeared a good match for the man the police were hunting. First off, there was his briefcase, which contained a length of rope, a jar of Vaseline, and a long-bladed knife. Then there was his record of sexual assaults against children, his ownership of the shack close to where Lena Zakotnova had been killed, and his resemblance to the man in the initial police identikit. Additionally, he was a perfect fit for the profile drawn up by Dr. Bukhanovsky. However, there was a problem. Chikatilo's blood type was A, and the police were certain that the killer was type AB.

Chikatilo was free to go. Soon after, Aleksandr Zanosovsky, the man who had arrested him, was criticized for his "overzealous pursuit" of the suspect and demoted.

In 1985, Chikatilo started a new job at a locomotive factory in Novocherkassk. This job involved travel, but his close shave with the law seems to have shaken him up. It was August before his urges once again overwhelmed him. While returning from a business trip to Moscow, he coaxed a mentally disabled girl from the train and stabbed her to death in the woods. Later that month, he picked up a girl at the bus station in Shakhty, led her into a wooded grove, and hacked her to death.

Chikatilo spent most of 1986 traveling the country. If he killed during this time, the murders went unrecorded. In May 1987, he stabbed a 13-year-old boy to death in the town of Revda in the Ural Mountains. In July, he killed another youth in Zaporizhzhia in Ukraine, and in September, another young boy perished at his hands, this time in Leningrad.

Nine more victims died in 1988, most of them while Chikatilo was on his travels. A notable exception was 16-year-old Tatyana Ryzhova. Chikatilo lured the girl to a vacant apartment in his hometown of Shakhty, plied her with vodka, and tried to have sex with her. Failing, as usual, to maintain an erection, he stabbed Tatyana to death, then mutilated her corpse, cutting out her uterus and slicing off part of her face.

The police had by now begun to notice ever more extreme mutilations to the corpses they recovered. Several were missing body parts, usually the uterus and nipples in females, the genitalia in males. In addition, the noses and tips of tongues were often sliced or chewed off, and the eyes were usually pried out. The victim profile was also changing. Chikatilo's early victims had been mainly female; seven of the last nine were boys aged between seven and sixteen.

On October 30, the police got another good description of their suspect after Chikatilo lured 16-year-old Vadim Tishchenko into the woods near Rostov's

Leskhoz train station and killed him. After Tishchenko's body was discovered, police officers questioned railway staff and found one who had seen the boy in the company of a tall, older man. The ticket seller said the man was a regular traveler, and he'd often seen him on the station trying to engage young people in conversation.

The net was closing on Andrei Chikatilo, but unfortunately, it didn't close fast enough to save his final victim. 22-year-old Svetlana Korostik was lured into the woods from Leskhoz station. There, she was beaten, stabbed, and mutilated. Chikatilo cut off the tip of her tongue and both nipples and ate them at the scene.

Following his usual M.O., he then covered the body with branches before walking back to the station.

This time, however, Chikatilo was spotted as he emerged from the woods. Questioned by police sergeant Igor Rybakov, he said that he'd gone into the trees to relieve himself. He insisted on boarding his train, which was waiting at the platform. The officer let him go, but not before making a note of his details. When Svetlana's body was found days later, Chikatilo was placed under surveillance. He was arrested on November 20 while trying to lure a young boy into the forest. The briefcase he was carrying contained a length of rope, a jar of Vaseline, and a knife with a long blade.

With Chikatilo in custody for a second time, the police did a more thorough forensic examination job. Hair and saliva samples were taken, and through them, it was discovered that Chikatilo was, in fact, blood type AB, the same as the killer. However, he fell into the small percentage of the population that are non-secretors. This means his blood has low levels of antigens, resulting in blood tests showing as type A.

Burakov finally had his man, but if he thought Chikatilo would be cowered or beaten into a confession, he was mistaken. Chikatilo stubbornly refused to speak, maintaining a stoic silence for nine days. Frustrated, Burakov turned again to Dr. Bukhanovsky, the psychiatrist who had so accurately profiled Chikatilo.

Bukhanovsky immediately honed in on a chink in Chikatilo's armor. He understood that Chikatilo's greatest concern was that his actions would shame his family. Bukhanovsky explained that they shouldn't be, as Chikatilo was mentally ill and therefore acting out of a compulsion that he could not control. He promised that he would explain this to Chikatilo's wife and family but that Chikatilo had to open up to him in order to do so. His confidence thus won, Chikatilo started talking.

The police had suspected Chikatilo of 36 murders. Now he stunned them by admitting to 56, describing in chilling detail how he'd raped, murdered, and brutalized his victims, sometimes devouring their body parts and drinking their blood.

In the months that followed, Chikatilo led detectives to crime scenes and burial sites across the country. His recall of details about murders committed a decade earlier astonished investigators, just as his obvious relish at describing his vile acts disgusted them. Chikatilo's death toll of 56 victims places him among the most prolific serial killers in history. He is certainly one of the most deprived.

Andrei Chikatilo went on trial on April 14, 1992, housed in a steel cage for the duration to protect him from the enraged members of his victims' families. During the three months that followed, proceedings were constantly interrupted by Chikatilo's bizarre rants. He complained about radiation and rats in his cell, declared that he was pregnant, and exposed himself to the judge and gallery on more than one occasion. At times he sat muttering to himself, and at others, he raged so violently that he had to be removed from the court.

But if it was an attempt at an insanity defense, it failed. Chikatilo was found guilty and, on October 15, 1992, sentenced to death.

Sixteen months later, on February 14, 1994, Andrei Chikatilo was put to death by a single bullet to the back of the head. Reportedly, the killer's final words were: "Don't shoot me in the head; the Japanese want to buy my brain."

13. Boone Helm (The Kentucky Cannibal)

Boone Helm, a man who traversed West America's mountains in the late 1800s, was dubbed as the "Kentucky Cannibal" because of his insatiable desire for human flesh. This flesh usually came from random people that he met during his travels.

Boone Helm was born on January 28, 1828, in the county of Lincoln, Kentucky. He was born into a family that had a good reputation in the community, although not very famous. At an early age, Helm and his family moved to Missouri. Helm, as a teenager, was known to be a boy that had the habit of displaying his bravado and "manliness." He would often ride his horse and performed several tricks, such as throwing a knife to the ground and picking it up while still riding the animal. There was also an occasion when Helm burst into a court proceeding that he was not a part of and verbally attacked the judge. Despite his rough behavior, he still ended up married. However, he continued to be a violent and inappropriate man. Helm was known to abuse his wife and would barge into establishments whilst riding his horse.

First Murder

Around the 1850s, when the gold rush in California broke out, Helm decided to go on a journey to try his luck in the goldfields. He frequently physically abused his wife, and he was a constant drain on his father's purse, so the decision to leave home was easy. Helm encouraged his cousin, Littlebury Shoot, to accompany him on the trip. Shoot initially said yes, but in the end, he changed his mind. The sudden change in plans angered Helm, which led him to commit his first murder. He repeatedly stabbed Shoot until he died. Helm was subsequently tried, but his behavior during the trial led the authorities to assume that he was not in his right mind and had a mental disorder. He was charged with murder, but Helm was sent to a lunatic asylum in California instead of spending his sentence in prison. During his stay in the asylum, Helm would trick the guard into allowing him to walk into the woods for him to clear and calm his mind. Apparently having a soft spot for the seemingly insane Helm, the guard would agree to his requests. On one occasion, however, Helm successfully escaped the asylum premises by beating the guard and escaping into the woods. From there, Helm fled in the direction of California and his original destination - the goldfields.

Succeeding murders

Following his escape from the asylum, Helm frequently journeyed through the mountains of California. During his trips, Helm obtained firearms, a horse, and some of the basic necessities of a mountain man. He would meet several random men during his journey and join their group or somehow lead his own. In this short but rather unlikely companionship, Helm would always be the one to challenge the men he met along the way. Sometimes, they would fight with their fists or with their guns and wouldn't stop until one of them lay dead. It is not known how many random men Helm killed.

On one of the routes, Helm followed, he and another man he had picked up met three miners near Keithley Creek. The said miners, who had already excavated a large amount of gold from the cave they had explored, were shot dead by Helm. Helm and his companion buried the gold that the miners possessed, and the miners' bodies were left on the road. He was deemed a suspect by the local authorities, and he fled to the northeastern mountains.

Cannibalism of Burton

After some time, Helm again gathered several companions – all with the common goal of reaching Idaho. However, the group encountered several problems. First, they were attacked by several Indians and who chased them into unknown territory. Second, the weather never cooperated, as Helm's group encountered several strong blizzards along the way. Although they somehow came out alive, all of their food had run out by the time they reached familiar terrain. The group gradually became fewer and fewer, the weak were left behind, and only those with enough energy left continued the journey. Eventually, only two men were left, Helm himself and a man named Burton. According to Helm, in a later confession, both he and Burton occupied an abandoned hut in the forest, but they didn't have any food left. While gathering firewood, Helm claimed to have heard a pistol fire. When he rushed back, he saw Burton's head had been blown to pieces; his companion had committed suicide. The authorities, however, suspected that it was Helm who killed Burton. Helm feasted on Burton's corpse, munching on the flesh of the man's extremities. When he was done, he chopped off the man's leg and carried it on his shoulder, a "food supply" that he kept for his next journey.

Hired Killer of the Mormons, Helm continued South where he met a kind rancher named John Powell. The rancher took care of him. Powell gave him clothes, food, and shelter, but Helm did not appreciate any of this. He wordlessly left Helm's house and headed to the Mormon settlements. He eventually became a hired killer for the Mormons. They paid Helm to kill people that they wanted to get rid of in exchange for money. His name gradually made the list of the suspects for unsolved murders, and he once again fled.

Murder and Cannibalism of Succeeding Companions Driven back to the wilderness, Helm found himself once again on a journey similar to those he had undertaken years before. He was still in search of more gold in Florence. Here, he was believed to have murdered and cannibalized a number of his companions. Dutch Fred, equally known as tough and violent a man as Helm, was murdered by the latter while unarmed. Helm was supposedly up for trial for murdering Fred, but his brother, known as "Old Tex," paid off all the witnesses. With all the witnesses gone, Helm got his freedom back.

Arrest and Execution

Helm continued to evade the law, and he joined Henry Plummer and his gang in a string of robberies and murders. The group was eventually arrested and tried. They were all found guilty, and Helm initially denied all the killings attributed to him. After being interviewed and even after Helm swore on the bible that he had not killed anybody in his life, he eventually admitted to the murders in California and Texas. He also admitted to eating Burton's remains and confessed that he would delightfully do so if given another opportunity to eat human flesh. Together with Henry Plummer's gang, Helm was executed in Virginia City, Montana, with around 6,000 people as an audience. At the execution, Helm told the executioners that he was not afraid to die. When he watched one of his friends about to be hanged, he told him that he'd be in hell too, after a minute. As the execution went on, Helm appeared to have gotten bored and jumped off the box to hang himself before his turn.

Conclusion

Now, we have come to the end of this series, and I'm sure you must have learned one or two things. Cannibalism is a crime, and you shouldn't be surprised if you have seen any of them. According to anthropologists, cannibals have always existed throughout human history: as a remedy for overpopulation, a means of survival during a famine, or even a way to cope with grief, virtually every civilization has devoured human people for some purpose at some point in time.

Murderers who kill for enjoyment and then consume their victims are uncommon. According to Dr. Eric Hickey, professor of forensic psychology at Walden University, between five and ten of the estimated 2,000 current serial killers in the United States are likely cannibals as well.

Cannibalistic killers tend to have a history of violence and rage that drives them to lash out and eat their victims. The source of their rage can be an abusive relationship with a parent, a tumultuous relationship with a lover or spouse, or the loss of a relative or spouse. Every time they attack and eat a victim, they release that rage, reliving their relationship and acting out vicariously at either an abusive parent or the other person in a troubled relationship.

By the same Collection:

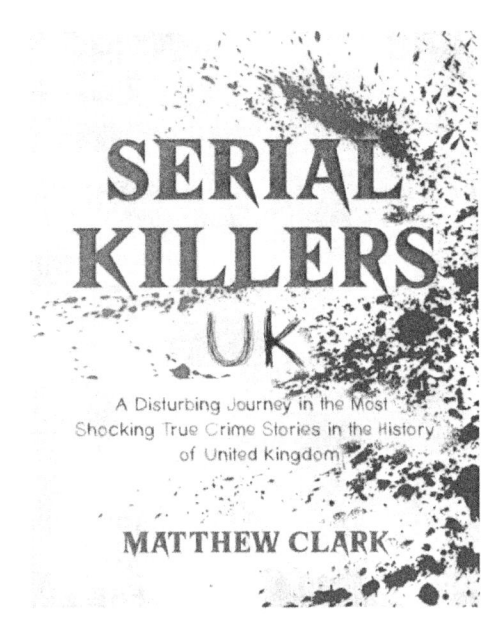

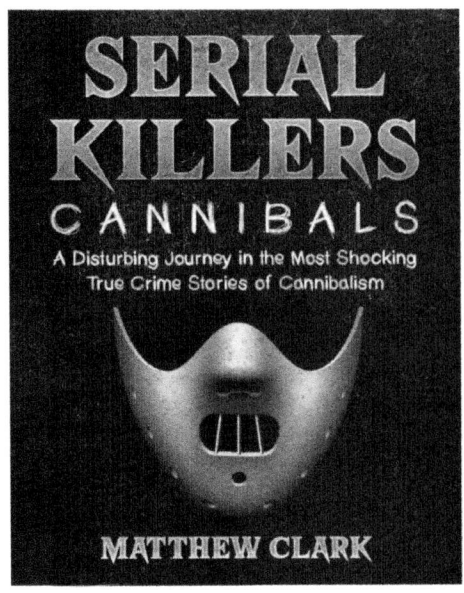

Search on Amazon!!

Printed in Great Britain
by Amazon